A VIEW
OF THE AMERICAN INDIANS

This is a volume in the Arno Press collection

AMERICA
AND
THE HOLY LAND

Advisory Editor
Professor Moshe Davis

Editorial Board
Professor Robert Theodore Handy
Professor Jules Davids
Dr. Nathan M. Kaganoff

See last pages of this volume for a complete list of titles.

A VIEW

OF THE

AMERICAN INDIANS

ISRAEL WORSLEY

ARNO PRESS

A New York Times Company

New York / 1977

E 61
.W67

Editorial Supervision: JOSEPH CELLINI

Reprint Edition 1977 by Arno Press Inc.

Reprinted from a copy in the American
  Jewish Historical Society Library

AMERICA AND THE HOLY LAND
ISBN for complete set: 0-405-10220-8
See last pages of this volume for titles.

Manufactured in the United States of America

Library of Congress Cataloging in Publication Data

Worsley, Israel, 1768-1836.
    A view of the American Indians.

    (America and the Holy Land)
    Reprint of the 1828 ed. printed for the author,
London.
    1. Indians--Origin. 2. Lost tribes of Israel.
I. Title. II. Series.
E61.W93 1977   970'.004'97   77-70757
ISBN 0-405-10303-4

In tribute to
DANIEL G. ROSS
for his leadership, friendship and counsel

A VIEW

OF THE

AMERICAN INDIANS,

POINTING OUT

THEIR ORIGIN.

A VIEW

OF THE

AMERICAN INDIANS

THEIR GENERAL CHARACTER, CUSTOMS, LANGUAGE,
PUBLIC FESTIVALS, RELIGIOUS RITES,
AND TRADITIONS:

SHEWING THEM TO BE THE DESCENDANTS OF

THE TEN TRIBES OF ISRAEL.

*The Language of Prophecy concerning them, and
the course by which they travelled from
Media into America.*

BY ISRAEL WORSLEY.

LONDON:

JUNE, MDCCCXXVIII.
PRINTED FOR THE AUTHOR, AND SOLD BY R. HUNTER,
ST. PAUL'S CHURCH-YARD, AND THE AUTHOR,
AT PLYMOUTH.

PRINTED BY W. W. ARLISS, PLYMOUTH.

CONTENTS OF THE VOLUME.

b

CHAPTER VIII.

CHAPTER IX.

CHAPTER X.

CHAPTER XI.

CHAPTER XII.

PREFACE.

THE subject that is treated of in these pages engaged the attention of the Inhabitants of the United States but too late, to obtain that clear investigation which is necessary for a full understanding of any subject. References to it and statements of facts which afford us an early light, are found in some of the public prints, and in Letters and Travels previous to the year 1816, when a volume was published at Trenton, New Jersey, by the Rev. Dr. Elias Boudinot, which bears for its title, *A Star in the West, or a humble attempt to discover the long lost Ten Tribes of Israel.* He gives the following account of himself and of his work.

'This subject has occupied the attention of the writer, at times, for more than forty years. He was led to the consideration of it, in the first instance, by a conversation with a very worthy and reverend clergyman of his acquaintance, who, having an independent fortune, undertook a journey, in company with a brother clergyman, who was desirous of attending him, into the wilderness between the Alleghany and Mississippi rivers, some time in or about the years 1765 or 6, before the white people

b 3

had settled beyond the Laurel Mountain. His desire was to meet with native Indians, who had never seen a white man, that he might satisfy his curiosity by knowing from the best source, what traditions the Indians yet preserved relative to their own history and origin. This, these gentlemen accomplished with great danger, risque and fatigue. On their return one of them related to the writer the information they had obtained, what they saw and what they heard.'

'This raised in the writer's mind such an idea of some former connection between these aborigines of our land and the Jewish nation, as greatly to increase a desire for further information on so interesting and curious a subject.'

'Soon after, reading (quite accidentally) the 13th chapter of the 2nd apochryphal book of Esdras, supposed to have been written about the year 100 of the Christian era, his ardour to know more of, and to seek further into the circumstances of these lost tribes, was in no wise diminished. He has not ceased since to improve every opportunity afforded him, by personal interviews with Indians, reading the best histories relating to them, and carefully examining our public agents resident among them, as to facts reported in the several histories, without letting them know his object; so as not only to gratify his curiosity, by obtaining all the knowledge relating to them in his power, but also to guard against misrepresentation as to any account he might thereafter be tempted to give of them. His design at present is, if by the blessing of Almighty God his life, now far advanced, should be spared a little longer, to give some brief sketches of what he has learned in this important inquiry, lest the facts he has collected should be entirely lost; as he feels himself culpable for putting off this business to so advanced a period of life, as to leave him but small hopes of accomplishing his intentions.'

In the year 1825 appeared another volume, written by Ethan Smith, Pastor of a Church in Poultney, 2nd Edn. entitled, *View of the Hebrews or the Tribes of Israel in America.* The great objection to these works, and especially the last, is their lengthyness, the profusion of matter which they contain, frequent repetitions, much of it foreign to the subject, and the disposition shewn to intermix religious views and party zeal, which cannot but be offensive to many readers.

The object of the present work is to extract from these and from other sources, as well as from the incidental remarks of our historians, Josephus, Prideaux, Gibbon, Robertson and others, such materials as bear directly upon the point in question, and to arrange them in a clear and concise manner, so as to give a short but conspicuous view of the subject. This has been found by no means an easy task, and may no doubt be improved if another edition should be called for; the materials of a work not being seen in a clear light until they have appeared in a connected form. The Author esteems himself particularly happy in having obtained a sight of a little Hebrew volume, the contents of which are given in the tenth Chapter. They furnish a most satisfactory support and form a valuable conclusion to the materials offered before them.

One of the most respectable authorities, for the manners and customs of this people since the time that they have become the object of attention to the moderns, is Mr. Adair's, who wrote a History of the Indians about the year 1775. He appears to have paid much attention to them, lived forty years domesticated with the Southern Indians, was a man of great respectability and learning, and left the States soon after he had prepared his manuscript, and escaped to England, on account of the troubles then coming on. This work was afterwards examined by a member of the Congress, who had acted as Indian Agent to the Southward, without his knowing the design of enquiring his opinion of it, and by him found to be correct in all its leading facts. Of this Mr. Boudinot made much use.

Charlevoix was a Clergyman of high respectability, who spent many years with them and travelled from Canada to the Mississippi at an early day. The Rev. Mr. Brainerd was a man of remarkable piety, and a Missionary to the Crosweek Indians to his death. Dr. Edwards was eminent for piety and learning and was intimately acquainted with them from his youth. Dr. Beatty, a Clergyman of note and established character. Bartram a man well known and respected, who travelled the country of the Southern Indians as a Botanist, a man of discernment and great means of knowledge : and M'Kenzie in the employment of the North-West company, an old trader, the first adventurous explorer of the country from the lake of the woods to the Southern Ocean.

It has been thought desirable to give in the first place a general outline of the character of the aborigines of America; which, to form a just opinion of them, should be taken from what was said or written about them by those persons who were acquainted with them in their original and pure state, before their alliance with Europeans induced new desires and new habits; and, from being the free unlicensed rangers in the vast woods and extensive Savannahs of the new world, they became persecuted and hunted hordes scattered by the pursuits of their invaders, or submitting with an abject and servile spirit to their laws, yielding to the bribery of intoxicating liquors, before unknown among them, and sacrificing each other to the lust and the vengeance of Europeans. The modern character of these wretched people has been indeed widely different from what it was when Columbus first sought their friendship, when Penn formed with them a just and friendly alliance, and when the persecuted and distressed Independents fled from the tyranny of a British Monarch, to seek liberty of conscience and the consolations of religion among a people, who, it will be my business to shew, had themselves fled from a tyrant's grasp, and, in a wide uncultivated, but rich and abundant country, of which they had gained intelligence, hoped to escape the pollutions of an idolatrous people, and worship their God in peace. The first in point of time of these objects, was fully obtained. No tyrant's law could restrain the wandering tribes in a country without inhabitants, capable of supporting hundreds of millions of people. But this very circumstance, of the wide range they were at liberty to take, was the cause of their being soon very widely scattered, as the tribes grew large and their families thickened, and of their losing that character of one people which marked them in the land of their captivity. Subject in their new abode to none but a patriarchal law, numerous circumstances would arise, many coincidences would take place, to give different characteristic features to the tribes and kingdoms which were formed among them; religious views and feelings would vary according as leaders of different minds rose up among them; and it may well be imagined, that while many customs of former times would remain to shew the relationship between them, some practices and some opinions would particularize their societies; so that after a lapse of some hundred years, they may be thought to have arisen from different heads. If I am correct in the point I have to establish, what more probable, than that the larger proportion of these rambling tribes would hold the belief in One God, whom they might with a striking truth and beauty call, The Great Spirit: while one body of them, retaining the Idolatrous impressions of their Assyrian master, would in the spirit of fear offer sacrifice to a Molock, the evil being, whom they had learned to regard as the Author of Evil and the power that had contaminated the beautiful creation and scattered curses over it: whom they must propitiate —and such were the Mexicans—and another body of them, entertaining more delightful views of the world and the author of it, would adopt the system of the ancient Magians; and, regarding light and fire as the image of God, and the symbols both of his purity and his beneficence, would adopt the bright luminary of day as their Emblem of the Almighty; believing with those ancient Sages, that the Sun was the place of his abode, the body which his

soul animated, and the great centre from which he scattered the rays of his love upon all the creatures of his formation—and such were the Peruvians: whose Incas were
the Children of the Sun: the first of them, they had been
taught to believe, had descended upon earth, a special gift
of their God, whose person and all whose race were sacred,
and received from them a subordinate worship. The three
great classes of the aboriginal Americans, first and best
known among them, bore these great and substantial marks
of a Hebrew and an Assyrian origin. By these marks
their forefathers in the land of Canaan had been distinctly
known: for their leanings towards Idolatry and some especial features of it, which I shall have occasion to point
out, are too plainly described in the scripture history to
leave us in any doubt; while they still professed, in a
defective manner, their belief in the One True God: and
probably their residence in Media of some continuance,
and how long we are not able with certainty to say,
little tended to lessen the disposition they had always
manifested to Idolatry, with its hateful and iniquitous customs. The Jews had never sunk so deep in that iniquity
which the holy soul of Jehovah abhorred, that they could
not be recovered: they were so to a great degree by their
captivity in Babylon. But of the tribes of Israel we have
never heard so good a character. Although the hands of
their forefathers were not stained with the blood of him whom
we, Christians, receive as the Messiah of God,—for they
were removed to a great distance from the scene of his
ministry, and did not fall under the temptation of thus
striving against God,—their habits were so deeply rooted,

their minds were so fast riveted to Idolatry, even of the vilest kind, that it must be believed many would retain those practices, and some would break out again in their new habitation and shew the indications of the disease deeply fixed in their race. There was not one King over the Israelites, after their separation from the house of David, who ruled the people according to the law of Moses: although therefore they had not altogether forsaken that law, yet they were well prepared to treat its injunctions lightly.

That their language should soon change and different dialects of it be formed, is no more than has occurred in all parts of the world upon the division of families. The three great heads of our race, the sons of Noah, separating from the place of their birth, in a Northern, an Eastern, and a Western direction, became the roots from which many nations sprang; and from them the numberless languages of the world have arisen. Many tongues are spoken by the inhabitants of Africa, many by the people of the East, and Sir William Jones, speaking of Tartars, says, that their languages, like those of America, are in perpetual fluctuation, and that more than fifty dialects are spoken between Moscow and China by the many hundred tribes and their several branches. Yet he has no doubt that they sprang from one common source. And it will further be shewn, that although the Indians have great and striking varieties in their language, yet all of them bear strong marks of being derived from one root. Of the first family he also observes, in his discourse on the origin of the Hindoos, Arabs and Tartars—" Hence it follows, that the only family after the flood established itself in the part now Persia, that as the family multiplied they were divided into three distinct branches, each retaining little at first, and losing the whole by degrees of their common primary language, but agreeing severally on new expressions for new ideas."

Manners soon degenerate amongst wandering tribes, living without principle, laws, education or civil government, especially where absolute want of the necessaries of life is sometimes taking place, and the necessity of doing without, causes the names and the uses to perish together. The Indian languages, not having been reduced to any certainty by letters, must have been exposed to great changes and to misconceptions. Our organs of speech do not act with an absolute certainty, and from a defect or a redundancy in any one of them, an object may obtain a new name or an idea may be conveyed by a different combination of sounds. The varied events of savage, as well as of social life, will have given rise to as varied a manner of speaking, and the mere caprice or authority of an individual will in many places have originated both words and phrases unknown to any others.

It will be seen in the perusal of the following pages that when the American Indians spoke of those places and persons that were selected for important national purposes and for those of religion, they invariably used a term expressive of high regard: their priests and old warriors were beloved men, their great square in which they met to celebrate public festivals was the beloved place, the hut or tent which contained the holy things was the beloved house. We cannot but feel pleasure at this

thought : for although the usages of social life would occasion such terms to appear affected on our lips, in a simple and unassuming state of society like theirs, the terms
convey a devotedness of mind to men experienced in life
and proved to be faithful, and to all that relates to the
Divine Being. I cannot but regard this simple circumstance as a beautiful trait of character, in those who have
been vilified in a thousand forms and shewn in the most
detestable points of light.

CHAPTER I.

ON THE ORIGIN OF MANKIND.   PLAN OF THE WORK.

DID we not know the rapacious disposition of mercan-
tile men when they leave their home in order to enlarge
their fortune and raise their families to wealth, it might
be thought a most extraordinary thing, that the settlers
on the western continent should have passed through a
long succession of years without giving themselves any
concern about the origin of the people among whom they
had settled and whose land they had seized upon; that a
race altogether different from any already found in any
part of the world should be within their knowledge and
under their eye, and yet no enquiry be made from what
stock they had descended, and in what branch they were
allied to the inhabitants of the old Continent.

The opinion generally prevailing among us is, that the
whole human race is descended from one pair.   This
opinion is derived from what we regard as divine authority;
but lest any of my readers should question that authority,
and conceive that the early part of the history of the world

was gathered by Moses or some other learned Israelite from traditions which had been handed down from generation to generation, and therefore do not bear a divine stamp; it shall be added, that this opinion is corroborated and strengthened, by the observations which have been made by philosophical observers on the different nations of the earth, by the light shades of difference which are perceptible in the gradations from the purest fair to the darkest black complexion, and the evident and palpable effects of climate, food, manners, customs, habit and education, the influence of superstition which has produced its effects on the body as well as on the mind of man, and a variety of political and moral regulations. If the mind be the standard of the man; it is not less true, that peculiar notions taken up and acted upon, have had a sensible influence on the features of the countenance, the motions of the body, the shade of complexion and other traits of the human character. So that although there are great diversities in the general appearance of mankind, and we may divide them into classes, each possessing peculiarities different from the others; yet are there none of these peculiarities, whether of form or feature, or colour, but may readily be accounted for by the influence of climate, food, &c. and this is yet more confirmed by the utter impossibility of drawing the line which shall separate one race from another, and decide that this is descended from the tawny race and that from the fair : because the difference is so small, while the similarity is so striking, that more easy would it be to divide the approximating colours of the rainbow. There are great dissimilarities observable in the Inhabitants of Europe; the nations of it are characterised in such a way as to be easily distinguished; the German, the Frenchman, the Dutchman, the Spaniard, although they have a general resemblance, are marked by traits wide enough to be known, as well in general appearance as in colour; nor can we readily say, why these nations have assumed peculiarities by which they are known among their fellows. But they have assumed those peculiarities. And if we pass over a few more leagues of the land or of the sea either to the north, the east, or the south, we come to nations whose complexions, whose form of countenance, whose figure, and whose manner of life, are very materially different from those of the European; yet, while they exhibit as many shades of difference as does the Iris on the cloud, they pass as gradually as do the colours of that beautiful bow from one to the other, which are known by differences so small, that we cannot perceive where one of these colours ends and another begins: so neither can we distinguish the termination of one set of characteristics of the human race and the beginning of another, so as to say, these are from one original stock and those from another.

The American tribes, of whom I am about to treat, have a general character peculiar to themselves, yet they differ in some striking particulars from one another. Their general resemblance has been observed by many persons who, independently of each other, have visited distant parts of that vast continent. There has been found a great likeness throughout, together with lines of difference, similar to those which are seen in the societies that possess the lands of the old hemisphere: but there are none of those great dissimilarities amongst them which mark the natives of Europe, Asia and Africa. Although they are spread over a country which bears a near proportion to the Eastern Continent, and stretches as wide from North to South, into the frigid and over the torrid zone, still a great resemblance is discovered among them, they have all the appearance of being descended from one stock.

When this extensive country became first known to the Europeans, it bore evident marks of having been but recently the abode of men. The greater part of it was wild, overrun with woods, interspersed with bogs and marshes, whose pestilential vapours the industry of man had not attempted to remove; extensive savannahs, in which wild herds of cattle fed undisturbed; and rivers to which those of Europe are streamlets, yet over which no vessels had ever sailed larger than the light canoe, made of the bark taken off sound and whole from their majestic trees, or cut out with uncouth instruments from the solid timber. It is a circumstance deeply to be regretted, that the first visiters of the new continent, and the first settlers upon it, do not appear to have entertained the thought of enquiring into the origin of this new people. At that period, before they were defiled by the impurities and the impieties of European civilization, and driven from their pacific settlements by European rapacities and cruelty, before they were scattered like sheep by ravenous wolves, and, being so scattered, lost gradually the marks by which they were then distinguished; and before they fell a sacrifice by hundreds and by thousands to the cruel bondage by which they were visited, to obtain for their unfeeling taskmasters that cursed gold which has enflamed the evil passions in all ages, but never before with that unfeeling rapacity that filled the Spaniard's breast with every unjust and impious thought—at that period much might have been discovered from the customs prevalent among them, and from the traditions which were fresh in their memories, and had not been disturbed by change of manners or by persecution, of their early history, and more certain means might have been obtained for tracing their origin. The Spaniards cared little for the history of these harmless people. They found them a set of beings different from the inhabitants of the old world, meek, peaceful, hospitable, benevolent, possessing few marks of what they regarded as civilization, and, compared with themselves in a state of ignorance and of barbarism. They found their interest in regarding and in describing them as an inferior race, and in the pride or the hypocrisy of their heart, they did not hesitate to declare, in the reports they sent home to their government, that they were of an inferior order of men, fitted only for beasts of burden. They forced them to toil in the rich streams that poured down from the mountains golden sand, they devoted them to labour in the mines which they soon discovered rising to the very surface of the mountains. Their only care was to blind the eyes of the rulers at home, to whom they were accountable for their conduct abroad; and so easily and so effectually did they complete this wicked purpose, that, by the misrepresentation of their wretched slaves, and the powerful influence of the silver and gold which they remitted to their king, they concealed the real condition, character, and powers of the natives from the Spanish Court, and went on for a long time in the exercise of rapacity, cruelty, and murder, until by far the greater part of the population of those territories which they had invaded were exhausted by rigorous treatment, by severe tasks which their delicate frame could not endure, and by a generally licencious conduct unchecked by any principle of humanity—but—alas—all in the name of religion!! These evils fell chiefly on those Americans who lived a comparatively civilized life—who had a quiet and a happy home, and, with few wants and those easily supplied, had no occasion for the bodily labours which stiffen the muscles and strengthen the nerves, and form the robust and vigorous man, and on that account were totally unfit for the hard duties imposed upon them by their merciless invaders. Happy were the wild and wandering tribes among them in those days of terror, who could strike their tents and retire into the woods at the sound of an enemy's footsteps. The savage as he was called was happy, while the civilized Indian fell a prey to the avarice and the reckless cruelty of the Spaniard. Long was it after these Christians had landed in America before, great as was their zeal for the catholic faith, they offered the consolations of religion to these wretched sufferers: and when at length they did offer them, it was with a view to enveigle, to deceive, and to pilfer them with greater ease. Yet the remarks which were made incidentally by some of the first settlers furnish valuable hints to support the object of the present work. Although they appear to have entertained no thought of these people being descended from an European or an Asiatic race, yet their observations tend in some instances to illustrate the subject which is now before us. Those remarks are the more valuable, because they came from observation, and without any thought the use that would afterward be made of them; and because they were made at the early period when the Americans retained more of their original character. In an enquiry like the present, some notion of the origin of the people is of great importance, because the enquirer will then have his mind directed to those traits of character which support his position; whereas, without it he may pass many of them by unobserved, for the want of perceiving their bearing on the point in view: and this was no doubt the case with the first settlers in America. They did not see the points of resemblance which we are now seeking for, because they had no conception of their existence, and their minds and their whole attention were turned to very different objects.

I may be lead astray in a contrary course. The man who thinks he is in possession of some new and valuable thought, and is desirous of establishing the proof of it, may exercise the energies of his mind to make all that occurs bend to support his opinion; in this way facts may be misrepresented or distorted for the express purpose of supporting an hypothesis. It may happen that circumstances will be detailed in this volume which have this character; for I shall not withhold even slight symptoms of resemblance which bear upon the point in question:

but, as I trust I shall produce much more than mere conjecture, many circumstances which amount to a strong presumptive proof, and an abundance of corroborating facts, those minor points of similitude will be regarded in their proper light, and be allowed to throw in their mite of evidence in support of the interesting fact, that—*The immense population with which the continent of America was found to be inhabited on its first discovery, were the direct lineal descendants of the nine tribes and a half, or a large part of them, that were carried captive by the Assyrian King, and since their banishment from their own country have been lost to their brethren the Jews and to all the historians of latter times.*

But can they be altogether lost, or can they be intermingled among the new tribes that have been formed and the new kingdoms that have sprung up? They constituted a large proportion, more than three fourths, of the chosen people of God; concerning whom so many prophecies stand recorded in the holy books, for whom so many striking interferences took place under the direct agency of the Almighty; for the express purpose of separating them from the idolatrous nations, of keeping them a distinct and peculiar people, of making them bear his name to the ends of the earth and spread his glory among the nations. Can they then be lost, destroyed, rooted out from the habitations of men? Or can they be so amalgamated with those Idolaters who conquered them, or with those people with whom they have since dwelt, as to be no more known a separate people, as to have lost their identity, and be no where to be found in the day to which the language of prophecy directs our attention, when those who have been *dispersed among the nations,* and those who have been CAST OUT, shall alike be called by the special voice of God to return to their country and city, to resume their power and dignity among the Kingdoms of the Earth, to en large and extend it yet farther than it was extended before, and to be settled finally and without relapse in the pure worship of Jehovah, whose name is one, and whose praise one?

Dean Prideaux seems to reconcile himself completely to the thought, that there has long been an end to those tribes. He says "thus the ten tribes which had separated from the house of David were brought to a full and utter destruction and never after recovered themselves." Again, "Some of these are said to have joined themselves to the Jews in Baylon and returned with them; whilst the mass of them, going into the usages and idolatry of the nations among whom they were planted, to which they were much addicted while in their own land, after awhile became wholly absorbed and swallowed up in them; and thenceforth utterly losing their name, their language, and their memorial, were never after any more spoken of." These are bold assertions for which the Dean produces no other proof, than that he, with other historians, have not discovered any satisfactory traces of them after that period.

The Jews are still a people, as distinct from all others as they ever were; they are if possible more distinct than ever. Intermixed with all the nations of the earth, according to the language of prophecy, dwelling among them, yet they connect themselves, in no religious or political alliance, with any of them. Favored by few, oppressed by many, still persecuted by some, like their forefathers in Egypt, they increase and multiply. Satisfied if they are allowed to remain quiet, they follow their own customs, while they submit to the laws of the state under which they live. But no privations—and they have suffered all that social man can suffer; no persecutions—and the cruelty of man has been taxed in many countries to discover and to invent engines of persecution to employ against them, have been able to turn them from their fidelity to that One Glorious Being whom they acknowledge as their God and King, and make them deny the faith which alone they believe to be of divine origin. Faithful people! Faithful to the light which has shone upon them, to the God who revealed himself to their parents of old! If they still are blind to the light which shone in our Messiah; if they deny him to be the messenger from their God, who was to call them from their backsliding and reveal to them his whole will, their forefathers in the time of the Saviour were blind to it before them, even when it was accompanied by signs, and wonders, and gifts of the Holy Spirit. This blindness was suffered to fall on them; it is still permitted to suffuse their minds, and to withhold their faith in Christ Jesus; and by the authority of an inspired pen we learn, it shall be so, until the fullness of the Gentiles be come in. Why it is thus, and how long it shall be so, rests with that Eternal Wisdom, to whom time has no divisions, with whom a thousand years are as one day. Under some impressions of christian credence they will be pitied, perhaps blamed: under others they will be respected: under none should they be ill used; and if we do but feel a conviction, that they act on a conscientious principle and do not become christians because they think they ought not, they do not deserve ill usage or reproach on our part more than we do on theirs, because we do not abandon our christian faith and submit to the Hebrew rites.

Their forefathers never sunk so deep in the iniquities of Idolatry as did their brethren of the ten tribes; but they often deviated from the true worship and defiled themselves with those sins which the righteous God abhors: for which abandonment of their integrity they incurred the penalty so often and so plainly denounced by the prophets. In the very peculiar state in which they continue to live we see the pledge and the certainty of their restoration.

Not less frequent nor less plain are the prophecies which were delivered to the Israelites while they dwelt in their own land. But they heeded them not; they went on in their sin, until the vengeance of Heaven was let loose upon them, the Avenger was brought up against them by that Being by whom kings reign, and they were carried captive to a strange land, there to expiate their sin by the suffering of distress and affliction, which were designed in the dispensations of Heaven to operate as a medicine to their diseased mind, and make them return with heart and soul to him from whom they had deeply revolted. If then this statement of the divine purpose be true, they cannot be destroyed, they cannot be mixed with the heathen, like the waters of a river in the great bed of the Ocean; they must still have an existence, as distinct as that of their brethren, the Jews, and will be found of him that seeks after them, when he shall display his great power and the banner of his salvation.

It is quite certain that in the captivity, both of the Jews and the people of Israel, the whole body of them was not included. Some were left behind, not worthy the captor's attention, others escaped before they were mustered to submit to their fate. Many, of those perhaps who had money at command, fled into Egypt. When Ptolemy, long after, obtained from the High Priest the copy of the holy writings, in order to have them translated into Greek, they were accompanied by a letter from Eleazar in which he wrote, "I have sent you six elders out of every tribe, with the law to attend your pleasure". Some of all the ten tribes must therefore have been at Jerusalem at that time: perhaps the holy city was never entirely without a few of every tribe.

The plan to be pursued in the present work is the following. We shall first take a view of the prophecies relative to the Tribes of Israel, both as to their dissolution and their recovery—then show the general character of the Inhabitants of the American Continent, the degenerate state to which they have been reduced, and the immense sacrifice of life they have sustained through the cupidity and licentiousness of the Europeans; their manners, customs and religious ceremonies; the traditions still found among them of their original settlement in that country, the people from whom they descended and the quarter at which their ancestors entered; the hopes and expectations which have been kept alive among them—and lastly, we shall attempt to trace the course which the ten tribes may be supposed to have taken, in order to arrive at this uninhabited but rich and luxuriant country. When these points have been investigated, and other remarks of an incidental nature laid before the reader, he will consider, whether there be not reason to believe, that the God of the Jews has still taken care of his chosen but rebellious people, that he still keeps them as the apple of his eye. On this point it is evident to remark, that in speaking of this race of men, both as to past, present and future time, it is the nation that is regarded; although many of the original families may have become extinct, the identity of the people remains, so long as they retain those marks of their origin which distinguish them as the people of God, and are unmixed with other families.

It would be unreasonable to expect that every difficulty that arises and every objection that may be started on this investigation will be entirely removed. It must be obvious to every person who considers the length of time since the captivity of the ten tribes of Israel, the wandering and destitute state of the Indian nations, their entire separation from all civilized society, their total ignorance of literature, the strange inattention of the Europeans who first settled among them to observe their modes of life, and the falsehood of those that did attempt it, the difficulty of obtaining a proper knowledge of their language, which has split into many dialects, together with the jealousy and fear they have entertained of the white people, from whom they have received little other than injury, extreme suffering and wanton destruction—It must be obvious that under such circumstances as these many difficulties will arise in this investigation. We have a comparison to make between a people originally possessing and observing a peculiar economy, but degenerating under that economy in an extreme degree, and intermixing in its laws and customs others to which they were originally and systematically hostile; calling themselves the worshippers of One God and yet indulging in the worship of many; acknowledging themselves bound to the Mosaic law yet uniting with it what was the most alien from it—and an immense population divided into separate communities, forming new kingdoms, instituting new laws; or remaining under the authority of no established code, but submitting to the rule of a chief who professed no authority but the tradition of which himself was the depository. When the very different states of two such people are considered, and the long lapse of time between the disappearance of the former and the discovery of the latter, together with the distance of the countries in which they severally resided, and that one was in the highest state of cultivation while the other was a wild waste: must it not be thought that, though these histories relate to the same people yet great and incalculable changes must have taken place among them, and that we are not to expect to find mauy clear and distinctive marks by which it may be made to appear, that the American Tribes are the offspring of the captivated and cast-out tribes of Israel.

CHAPTER II.

OF THE PROPHECIES.

FROM the history of the Hebrews and from their sacred writings it appears, that the great Governor of the universe did select that people from all the nations of the earth, not only to receive and to preserve the great doctrine of the divine Unity, together with that purity and singleness of worship which he requires; but also to deliver over the same to the other nations. They have been made the depositories of Prophecies, instructive not to themselves alone but to all the earth. They were early informed, in a language the most plain, what would befal them in future years, according as they kept the commandments of God or were disobedient to them, and in their rebellion they fully experienced the truth of the prophetic words. Moses seems to have been perfectly acquainted with the untoward disposition of the people when he brought them out of the land of Egypt, and how great their tendency would be to revolt to the absurdities and abominations of the nations around them; and being inspired with a spirit of prophecy, he warned them of their danger in sublime language. Deut. 4. 23. "Take heed to yourselves lest ye forget the covenant of the Lord your God which he made with you, to make you a graven image or the likeness of any thing which the Lord thy God hath forbidden thee. For the Lord thy God is a consuming fire. —When you corrupt yourselves and make a graven Image I call Heaven and Earth to witness against you this day, that ye shall soon utterly perish from off the land whither ye go over Jordan to possess it. And the Lord God shall scatter you among the nations, and ye shall be left few in number among the heathen, whither the Lord shall lead you. And ye shall serve other Gods, the work of men's hands, wood and stone, which neither see, or hear, nor eat, nor smell. But if from thence thou shalt seek the Lord thy God, thou shalt find him, if thou seek him with all thy heart and with all thy soul."

After this Moses gave them the law, and enumerated many blessings which should be conferred on them in case of their hearkening diligently to the voice of the Lord, to observe and do his commandments, and then passed on to the extraordinary and dreadful curses which would rest upon them if they were disobedient to the heavenly vision. See 29. 10. and following.

For the fulfilment of the divine commands it was necessary to separate them from the rest of the people of the earth; so that their political and religious institutions might be known to the world, and the exclusive nature of their principles. They were thus separated, and enjoyed the privileges of their land through many generations: but ᴄᴇy soon forgot the covenant of their God and fell into the Idolatry of other nations. About seven hundred years before the christian era, near the time of Salmanazar, King of Assyria, Isaiah the prophet rose among them and delivered from God this solemn message. "The Lord sent a word unto Jacob and it lighted upon Israel, and all the people shall know, even Ephraim and the inhabitants of Samaria, who say in the pride and stoutness of their heart, the bricks are fallen down but we will build with hewn stone &c.—therefore the Lord will cut off from Israel head and tail, branch and root, together." Isaiah 9. 8 to 19. "O Assyrian! the rod of mine anger; and the staff in their hand is mine indignation. I will send him (the Assyrian), against an hypocritical nation, and against the people of my wrath will I give him a charge, to take the spoil and to take the prey and to tread them down as the mire of the streets." ch. 10. 5. 6. In ch. 11 11. is a promise that he will recover his people from their bondage though scattered in every place; among others *from the western regions* according to Lowth, improperly rendered in the received version, the islands of the Sea. "And he shall lift up a signal to the nations, and shall gather *the outcasts of Israel* and *the dispersed of Judah* from the four extremities of the earth. And there shall be a highway for the remnant of his people which shall remain trom Assyria."

In these words we discover a marked difference between the fate of the Jews, who in the language of Scripture are called Judah, and comprise the tribes of Judah and Benjamin, that adhered faithfully to the house of David;

and the other ten tribes usually called Israel, and also Ephraim, who had served another race of kings. The one is described as dispersed among the nations in the four corners of the globe, the other as outcasts from the nations. This restoration is said to be accomplished a second time. The first was from Egypt, the second from all parts to which they were spread. The places too are designated from whence they shall return, from Assyria and Egypt, where many of the Jews still reside, from different parts of Persia, where are numbers of them, from the provinces of Assyria, and from the *western regions*. The two tribes of Judah and Benjamin, which are well known to be still dispersed throughout the three quarters of the Globe, are thus distinctly described, together with the places in which they will be found; with whom a part of the tribe of Levi have always been intermixed—but as for the majority of these privileged people, the nine tribes and the rest of the Levites, generally known by the designation of the ten tribes, although the devout believer in divine revelation has no doubt of their being preserved by the sovereign power of God in some unknown region, yet, after the world has been traversed in every possible direction, they have not yet been discovered. The interpretation given by Lowth, who when he wrote his translation of Isaiah, had no thought of the subject now before us, directs us to look for them in the *western region* whither they had been *cast out.*

The passages in Isaiah which have a reference to God's people are numerous, I need not repeat them all, but would refer my reader also to the forty-third chapter at

the beginning, "But now saith the Lord who created thee,
O Jacob, and he who formed thee, O Israel; fear not for
I have redeemed thee, &c. In Is. 49. 12 they are described as passing mountains from far and coming from
the north and west and others from the eastern country.
In the book of Ezekiel 37. 16. we have this striking
passage, "Moreover, thou son of man, take thee a stick
and write upon it, 'for Judah and for the children of Israel,
his companions." And then another stick and write upon
it, 'For Joseph, the stick of Ephraim and for all the house
of Israel, his companions.' And the fact has been as the
prophet intimated: for at the captivity some of the people
of Israel were intermixed with those of Judah and taken
away with them, while the greater part were carried captive at a different time and placed in a country to the
north of Babylon.

The return of these tribes has also an allusion to them
as a separate people, Zech. 8. 7. "I will save my people
from the east country, from Babylon and Assyria, and
from the west country". I should also refer the reader to
the 20th. Ezekiel, 35 and following verses, from which it
appears, that they will be gathered out of all countries
whither they have wandered, and *from a wilderness* in
which God will plead with them, that they will suffer
greatly, and yet with reluctance will leave their settlement, and their return shall be in many respects like that
of their fathers out of Egypt. It is not possible for language to be more clear than is the language found in many
of the prophets, of the final return of these tribes to their
former city and country; which language is not confined

to the Jews, who are known still to exist in great numbers; but equally applies to the Israelites. Ezekiel writes, "Thus saith the Lord, behold I will take the children of Israel, (these terms are applied to the whole family of Jacob,) from among the heathen, whither they are gone, and will gather them on every side, and bring them into their own land, and I will make them one nation in the land upon the mountains of Israel, and one king shall be king of them all, and they shall no more be two kingdoms any more at all." Ez. 37. 21. and the following verses. They are especially charged with the sin of drunkenness, of which more will be said hereafter.

Amos was of the ten tribes and delivered his prophecies not long before their banishment. There is an extraordinary correspondence between his prophetical words and those of Esdras which were historical. He describes the Idolatry of Israel, thus, "They that swear by the sins of Samaria, and say, Thy God, O Dan, liveth; and the manner of Beersheba liveth: even they shall fall." Those two places were at the extremes of Samaria, Chap. 8. 11 and following. "Behold the days come, saith the Lord, that I will send a famine on the land—on the tribes of Israel—not a famine of bread, nor a thirst of water; but of hearing the word of the Lord. And they shall wander from sea to sea and from the north even to the east, they shall run to and fro to seek the word of the Lord, and shall not find it." Here is a prediction, that in their exile they shall know, that they were blessed with divine communication but have lost it; which correctly corresponds with declarations of ten made by the Indians to the

Europeans—that they shall rove from sea to sea and from *the north even to the east*—the exact course which it will be shewn they took—from the Mediterranean to the eastern ocean, and again from the Pacific to the Atlantic Ocean: they shall run to and fro through a large and free space, they shall retain some just notions of God, and seek his word from their priests, but shall not find it. In the 15th. their return is foretold. "I will bring again the captivity of my people Israel &c." The spirit of prophecy has thus furnished us with a valuable clue to the discovery of those tribes : not in their own land nor scattered among the nations—but passing from the north to the east and from sea to sea, roving about; retaining some traditionary views of former things, seeking divine communications, but in vain. When the pages of this volume have been read, their traditions considered and their usages surveyed, it is not too much to say, that the tribes of Israel will be recognised in America, perishing under the predicted famine of the word.

The language of prophecy must be acknowledged to be of difficult interpretation, and it is only where the terms of it do appear to apply clearly to any particular case that I should be disposed to attempt its explanation. Now some of those of the prophets seem to deserve notice on the subject that is before us. Let the reader turn also to the thirtieth and thirty-first chapters of Jeremiah, which were written about a hundred and twenty years after the expulsion of the ten tribes, he will find promises which have not yet been fulfilled, a restoration *in the latter days*. They are called *Ephraim, my dear Son* "upon whom the

Lord will have mercy : he will bring again the captivity of his people and cause them to return to the land of their fathers, he will save them from afar, and gather them from the coasts of the earth, because they called thee an outcast, saying, this is Zion, whom no man seeketh after." He speaks of *Isles afar off*, which signify lands beyond sea. See also ch. 16. and Isaiah 18. " Ho, thou land shadowing with wings"—an illusion perhaps to the safety in which the people shall rest in that unmolested country—" which is beyond the rivers of Ethiopia. Who sendest Embassadors by the sea, even in vessels of bulrushes upon the face of the waters," a nation expert in navigation. "Go ye swift Messengers to a nation scattered and peeled, whose land the rivers have spoiled." Rivers is a prophetic term often used for armies which overflow a country. Verse 7. "At that time shall a present be brought of a people scattered and peeled &c."

There are numerous other chapters in the prophets to which the reader might be referred, which speak of the return of the Israelites, as well as of the Jews, to their own land at a future period, sufficiently plain to convince us, that they have been kept by the mighty power of God, and still are preserved, against that great day of their salvation. But where in all the world can they be found if it be not on the Continent of America ?

In the forty-ninth chapter of Isaiah, the prophetic language is of a peculiar cast and although I will not say it distinctly points to a Country and people situated as America and its inhabitants are, yet I must not omit directing the attention of my readers to its contents. It

begins with an invocation to the Isles—which term does
not appear to mean land surrounded by water, but land
afar off which can be reached only by crossing water—
"Listen, O Isles, unto me and hearken ye people, from
far." This is the language of the people of Israel. "He
said unto me, thou art my servant, O Israel, in whom I
will be glorified." The prophet then speaks of raising up
the tribes of Jacob, and restoring the preserved of Israel:
that in an acceptable time he heard them and in a day of
salvation he delivered them: to the prisoners he would
say. "Go forth, and to them that are in darkness, shew
yourselves. Behold, these shall come from far, from the
north and from the west." Zion is then made to lament
that the Lord had forgotten her; and an assurance is
given, that should a mother forget her suckling child yet
the Lord will not forget her, and that the numbers which
shall return to her will be so great that the land now
desolate will be too narrow by reason of its inhabitants.
Then follows. "The children which thou shalt have,
after thou hast lost the other."—the race of the Jews,
after they had long lost their brethren the Israelites shall
say, "the place is too strait for me give place that I may
dwell." "Then shalt thou say in thine heart. Who hath
begotten me these, seeing I have lost my children, and
who hath brought up these? Behold I was left alone!
These, where have they been?" After which we learn
that the ruling powers of nations shall be employed to
restore the people of God, who had been utterly out of
sight of the Jews during the period of their dispersion.
In the 53 chapter we have a description of these people in

their outcast banished state claiming the Lord for their God "Doubtless thou art our father though Abraham be ignorant of us and Israel acknowledge us not, thou, O Lord, art our father, our redeemer, thy name is from everlasting." Here then is a branch unacknowledged by those who have been always acknowledged as Jews, and yet claiming their privileges as descendants of Abraham. When these tribes shall know, from their own traditions or by other means which the Almighty will employ to bring them in, that they are the descendants of the ancient people of God, this is language befitting their situation : as is also that which follows. "O Lord why hast thou made us to err from thy ways and hardened our hearts from thy fear ? Return for thy servants' sake, the tribes of thine inheritance."

A violent enmity had subsisted between Judah and Israel ever since the separation of the latter from the family of David—but this enmity is to cease, "The envy of Ephraim shall depart: Ephraim shall not envy Judah and Judah shall not vex Ephraim," This passage assures us of the restoration of Israel. Is. 11. 13.

There is a passage in Hosea 4. 16. which confirms and illustrates the subject. For although the Lord had determined to let them alone for a long period when they were joined with idols; yet it is said "The Lord will feed them as a lamb in a large place." This is a declaration that cannot be said of the Jews—who instead of being treated with the mildness which a lamb requires, have been every where harassed, worried and afflicted; but of the other tribes, it may be said, that he has fed them with a shepherd's care in a large place.

CHAPTER III.

GENERAL CHARACTER OF THE ORIGINAL AMERICAN
TRIBES.

To give a just description of a people so widely spread, and divided by thousands of miles from each other, having of course different habits prevailing among them, cannot be an easy task; and it is become so much more difficult at the present time, from the great changes which have taken place among them by their alliance with Europeans, and their having adopted more or less of their manners. Had these unfortunate outcasts from civilized society been favored at the first discovery of their country with inquisitive, learned and disinterested historians, who would have represented their characters fairly, we should have seen them in a very different point of light from that in which they now are seen. Some of their customs have appeared barbarous and even brutal to civilized people; yet, if compared with the conduct of the nations of the Eastern Continent, the balance would on the whole be in their favour. A great outcry has been made about their thirst

D

of blood; but by whom has this outcry been made? By the very people who in their contests with each other upon that continent have used every means to engage the natives to take part with them, and have encouraged them to fight in their own way, who have furnished them with tomahawks, scalping knives, muskets, powder and ball, and have enflamed their passions to the utmost by spirituous liquors, feasts and harangues, to increase their thirst of blood and drive them to the destruction even of their own brethren. The Europeans have made them savages and then have called them so.

When America was first discovered by Columbus it was peopled by hundreds, probably by thousands of tribes or nations. Their numbers have not been known, nor can they be known at this day. An alphabetical list is given in Pike's Expedition, of the tribes in the North, amounting to one hundred and ninety, each having a Sachem or King over them. The dialects of these nations differed greatly; a circumstance which has often happened among people without education and writing of any kind, separating and living at a distance from one another. The Erigas a tribe on the Ohio, who separated from the Tuscororas, are known to have formed a distinct dialect in the course of a few years.

Dr. Williams, in his history of Vermont, writes: "In whatever manner this part of the earth was peopled, the Indians appear to have been the most ancient or the original men of America. They had spread over the whole continent from the fiftieth degree of north latitude to the southern extremity of Cape Horn. And these men every where appear to be the same race or kind of people. In every part of the continent, they are marked with a similarity of features colour and every circumstance of external appearance." Pedro de Leon, one of the conquerors of Peru, who had travelled through many provinces of America, says of the Indians, "The people, men and women, although there are such a multitude of tribes or nations, in such diversities of climate, appear nevertheless like the children of one father and mother." The same testimony, of the striking likeness of one with other nations of them, is borne by all who have visited different tribes. But this remark does not apply to the Esquimaux, who appear to be a different race. Those which are found in Labrador, Greenland and round Hudson's Bay, are said to resemble the Laplanders, Samoyeds and Tartars, who may have gone over from the north of Europe to Iceland and thence to Greenland and Labrador. These people do not seem to have intermixed with the Indians.

Du Pratz, in his history of Louisiana, gives an account of the nation of the Paducas, west of the Missouri, in 1724, which may furnish a faint idea of the numbers originally inhabiting this vast continent. He says "The nation of the Paducas is very numerous, extending about two hundred leagues: they have settlements quite close to the Spaniards of New Mexico. They have large villages which are permanent abodes, from which a hundred hunters set out at a time, with horses, bows, and a good stock of arrows. The village in which we were consisted of one hundred and forty huts, containing eight hundred warriors, fifteen hundred women, and at least two thousand children; some men having four wives."

Some writers report the number of the warriors in the state of Virginia to have been fifteen thousand, and their population fifty thousand, each village containing fourteen thousand souls. From which it is but a moderate estimate to suppose, that there were six hundred thousand fighting men or warriors on this continent at its first discovery. Various estimates of this kind were made by different persons long time ago, under the direction of the government, and by the Missionaries sent among them.

Of the Mexican Indians we learn, that according to their account the empire had not been of long duration. Their country was rather possessed than peopled by small independent tribes, whose mode of life and manners resembled that of the most rude: that, about the period corresponding with the beginning of the tenth century, many tribes moved in successive emigrations towards the north-west, and settled in what is now called New Spain. These began to form themselves to the arts of social life. Long after they were united they were unacquainted with regal dominion, and were governed in peace and conducted in war by such as were entitled to pre-eminence by their wisdom or their valour; whose authority centered at last in a single person. From the migration of their parent tribes they reckoned only about three hundred years; from the establishment of the monarchy a hundred and thirty, or two hundred by another computation.

The colour of the Indians, generally speaking, is red, brown or copper colour, differing according to climate and to high or low ground. They are universally attached to their colour, thinking it an honourable mark of distinction. They make use of stains, prepared from plants and trees, to deepen it.

The powerful operation of heat appears to be the cause which produces the striking varieties in the complexion of men. All Europe, great part of Asia, and the temperate parts of Africa, are inhabited by men of a white colour, with varieties proportioned to the heat: the torrid zone of Africa, and some spots of Asia, are filled with blacks; the colour increasing as we advance towards the meridian, and deepening till it becomes perfectly black. In Africa the colour is the deepest of all in consequence of the extensive deserts of sand and the intense burning heat which they induce. But in America the same phenomena are not seen; a little difference of colour is perceptible as we advance to the southward, but a striking similarity is found in the figure and general aspect of the people. This difference of the influence of climate in the two continents is accounted for by Robertson, by "the intense cold which comes from the pole where reposes an eternal body of snow and ice, the influence of which on the atmosphere is not completely overcome even when it reaches the gulf of Mexico." To which may be added as a cause of the difference, the still defective cultivation of the land, the immense swamps in the neighbourhood of the great rivers, and the want of the burning sands which cover a large part of the other continent. I scruple not also to add the fact of the recent population of that extensive country by one of the great families of mankind.

The testimony of so great a historian as Robertson on this point we must not omit: excepting the Esquimaux and Greenlanders, he says, "Among all the other Americans there is such a striking similitude, in the form of their bodies and qualities of mind, that notwithstanding the diversities occasioned by climate and an unequal progress in improvement, we must believe them descended from one scource. Variety of shades, but all one colour; each tribe something to distinguish it, but all certain features common to the race:" after some other remarks he compares them to the rude Tartars, "from whom I suppose them to have sprung." "The Esquimaux and the dwellers round Hudson's Bay, to whom the Greenlanders may be added, are the only people of America that are unlike the main body, and bear a resemblance to the Europeans. Of the origin of those people we are instructed by Grotius, that "some of the Norwegians passed over into America by way of Greenland."

Proud of their red colour, to the white people the natives give names expressive of contempt: often with great bitterness they call them, "the accursed people." It is asserted by Adair, from actual observation, that the hotter the country in which they dwell, the deeper is the colour of their bodies. They endeavour every where to cultivate the copper colour, but some are naturally fairer than others. They have a tradition among them, that in the country far west, from which they came, all the people are of one colour, but they no longer know what that colour was. Europeans have been known to become as deeply coloured as the Indians, by living among them and using the means they furnished them with, in a very few years. The inhabitants of the north are not of so deep a dye as those of the south, a fact which is as observable in Europe and Asia as it is in America.

It is a matter of fact proved by historical documents, that the Europeans found these people upon their first intimacy kind, hospitable and generous ; wanting nothing themselves, they were ready to communicate of their plenty to others : but when through a thirst of gain, they were over-reached and betrayed, and their friends and relatives were stolen away and sold to slavery, an inveterate enmity and a spirit of revenge succeeded to their natural kindness. The evil passions, cruel conduct, and vicious habits which afterwards distinguished them, are to be attributed, not to themselves, but to those who forced them into birth: their conquerors raised their jealousy, provoked their free spirit, and furnished all the means of propagating and spreading the evil.

Take but the account given by Dr. Robertson of the hostilities carried on in the colony of Virginia. "So much were the natives provoked by the conduct of the new settlers who were few and feeble, that they formed the determination to extirpate them. Their attack was conducted with secrecy, the colonists were surprised and a large proportion of them were cut off. In their turn the survivors waged a destructive war with the Indians, and regardless, like the Spaniards, of those principles of faith, honor, and humanity, which regulate hostilities among civilized nations, the English deemed every thing allowable which helped to accomplish their designs. They hunted the Indians like wild beasts rather than like men ; and as the approach to them in the woods was difficult and dangerous, they allured them from their fastnessses with offers of peace and promises of oblivion, and with such an artful appearance of sincerity as deceived the Indian chief, and induced them to return in the year 1623 to their former settlements, and resume their peaceful occupations. The behaviour of the two people seemed now to be reversed. The Indians, like men acquainted with the principles of integrity and good faith, confided in the reconciliation and lived in security, without suspicion of danger; while the English, with perfidious craft, were preparing to outdo the savages in cruelty and revenge. On the approach of harvest, when a hostile attack would be most fatal, the English fell on the Indian Plantations, murdered every person of whom they could lay hold, and drove the rest into the woods, where great numbers perished through want; and some of the tribes which were nearest the coast were totally extirpated."

Of the war in New England, in their first attempt against the Pequod Indians he writes thus: "The Indians had secured their town, which was on a rising ground on a swamp, with pallisades; The New England troops unperceived reached the pallisades ; the barking of a dog alarmed the Indians. In a moment they started to arms, raised the war-cry and prepared to repel the assailants. But the English forced their way through into the fort, set fire to the huts which were covered with reeds, and confusion and terror soon became general. Many women and children perished in the flames, and the warriors who endeavoured to escape were either slain by the English or falling into the hands of their Indian Allies, were reserved for a more cruel fate. The English resolved to pursue their victory, and hunting the fugitives from one place to another, subsequent encounters were scarcely less fatal than the first action: and in less than three months the tribe of the Pequods was extirpated."

He also states "that the inhabitants of the islands resembled very much those of the main land in their appearance and manner of life: but the Carribbees are said to have been canabals, which charge has also been brought against the inhabitants of Rio Plata." This may be one of the calumnies brought against them by their enemies and invaders, to blacken them, and give a kind of justification to their own cruel treatment and plan of extermination, and might arise from the solemn and formal manner in which they execute some that have been taken in war, to satisfy the ashes of friends on whose account the war had been carried on.

"Thus the English stained their laurels by the use they made of victory. Instead of treating the Pequods as an independent people, who made a gallant effort to defend the property, the rights, and the freedom of their nation, they retaliated upon them all the barbarities of American war, to which themselves had first given birth. Some they massacred in cold blood, others they gave up to be tortured by their Indian Allies, a considerable number were sold as slaves in Bermuda, the rest were reduced to servitude among themselves." It has been in this way, it is to be feared, that the larger part of that ground on which the Independent States of America are now boasting of their freedom, was first obtained from its former owners and finally secured to the present possessors.

If the character of the Indians, as originally kind and hospitable, should be doubted by those who would judge of them by their more recent circumstances and conduct; we may go back to the days of Columbus, and learn what he thought of them: no one surely could be a better judge of the native character of that unknown people. In writing to his master, the King, under whose sanction he made his voyage, he says, "I swear to your Majesties, that there is not a better people in the world than these, more affectionate, affable and mild. They love their neighbours as themselves. Their language is the sweetest, the softest and most cheerful, for they always speak smiling."

A venerable old man one day approached Columbus with great reverence, and presenting him with a basket of fruit, said, "You are come into these countries with a force against which, were we inclined to resist, resistance would be folly. We are all therefore at your mercy. But if you are men, subject to mortality like ourselves, you cannot be unapprised, that after this life there is another, wherein a very different portion is allotted to good and bad men. If therefore you expect to die, and believe with us, that every one is to be rewarded in a future state, according to his conduct in the present, you will do no hurt to those who do none to you."

De Las Casas, Bishop of Chapia, who spent much time and labour among the Indians of New Spain, writes,

"I was one of the first who went to America, neither curiosity nor interest prompted me to undertake so long and so dangerous a voyage. The saving the souls of the heathen was my sole object. It was said, that barbarous executions were necessary to punish or check the rebellion of the Americans. But to whom was this owing? Did not this people receive the Spaniards who first came among them with gentleness and humanity? Did they not shew more joy in proportion, in lavishing treasure upon them, than the Spaniards did greediness in receiving it? Though they gave up to us their lands and riches, we would also take from them their wives, their children, and their liberty. To blacken the character of these unhappy people, their enemies assert that they are scarcely human beings. But it is we who ought to blush, for having been less men and more barbarous than they. They are represented as a stupid people and addicted to vice. But they have contracted most of their vices from the examples of christians. The Indians still remain untainted by many vices usual among Europeans, such as ambition, blasphemy, swearing, treachery, which have not taken place among them. They have scarcely an idea of these, &c."—Similar representations are given by Spaniards who had the earliest opportunites of knowing these people; although it has ever been a subject of deep regret that the public authorities who were sent out by the Spanish Government, and even many of the priests who accompanied them, made it a business to vilify these poor creatures, and represent them as fit only to be employed as beasts of burden.

In a sermon which was preached at Plymouth, in the year 1620, by the Rev. Mr. Cushman, the following remarks are found: "The Indians are said to be the most cruel and treacherous people, even like lions, but to us they have been like lambs; so kind, so submissive, so trusty, as a man may truly say, many christians are not so kind and sincere. Though when we first came into this country we were few, many of us very sick and many died by reason of the wet and cold, it being the depth of winter, and we having no house or shelter, yet when there were not six able persons among us, and the Indians came daily to us by hundreds with their Sachems or Kings, and might in one hour have made dispatch of us, yet they never offered us the least injury in word or deed."

Many are the authorities which might be quoted to shew the simplicity, amiableness, and excellence of the character these people manifested upon the first settlement of the Europeans on the eastern coast of North America, and in many parts where they were not provoked to desperation for a century afterwards; but, as much has been written as is necessary for the purpose that is now before us. One quotation more will carry our views into the back settlements, where we shall find tribes of people bearing the same characteristics. Father Charlevoix travelled at an early period and spent a long time among them, traversing the country from Quebec to New Orleans, and had no object in view but to study and improve the character of his hosts. He writes of them thus:

"With a mien and appearance altogether savage, and with manners and customs which savour of the greatest barbarity, they enjoy the advantages of society. At first view one would imagine them without form of government, laws or subordination, and subject to the wildest caprice. Nevertheless they rarely deviate from certain maxims and usages founded on good sense alone, which holds the place of law and supplies in some sort the want of legal authority. They manifest much stability in the engagements they have solemnly entered into; patience in affliction, as well as submission to what they apprehend to be the appointment of providence. In all this they manifest a nobleness of soul and constancy of mind at which we rarely arrive, with all our philosophy and religion. They are slaves neither to ambition nor interest, the two passions which have so much weakened in us the sentiments of humanity, and kindled those of covetousness, which are as yet generally unknown to them."

"What surprises exceedingly in men whose outward appearance proclaims nothing but barbarity is, to see them behave to each other with a kindness that is rarely met with in civilized nations, a natural and unaffected gravity, which reigns in all their behaviour and even in their diversions; especially the deference that is always shewn by young people to the aged: and never to see them quarreling or using those indecent expressions, those oaths and curses, so common in most communities." Du Pratz says of them, "I have attentively considered these Indians a long time, and never found or heard of any disputes or boxings with either boys or men." In short, says Boudinot, "to make a brief portrait of these people, with a savage appearance, manners and customs,

E

which are entirely barbarous, there is observable among them a social kindness, free from almost all the imperfections which so often disturb the peace of a civil society. They appear to be without passion, but sometimes do that in cold blood, and even through principle, which unbridled passion produces in those who give no ear to reason. We discover in them a mixture of the fiercest and most gentle manners: the imperfections of wild beasts and the virtues of the heart and mind which do the greatest honour to human nature."

"The nearer view we take of our savages, the more we discover in them some valuable qualities. The chief part of the principles by which they regulate their conduct, the general maxims by which they govern themselves, and the bottom of their characters have nothing appearing barbarous. The ideas, though now quite confused, which they have retained of a first Being; the traces though almost effaced of a religious worship, which they appear formerly to have rendered to the Supreme Deity, and the faint marks which we observe even in their most indifferent actions of the ancient belief and the primitive religion, may bring them more easily than we think of into the way of truth, and make their conversion to christianity more easily to be affected than that of more civilized nations."

Accounts very similar to these, representing the natives as amiable and highly estimable, are also given by Du Pratz in his history of Louisiana, and by Mr. Bartram, son of John Bartram, Esq. Botanist to Queen Caroline, who visited the Creek nation inhabiting the vast territory of East and West Florida.

Such are some of the ideas of the Indian character on the arrival of the Europeans among them, before they were debauched and demoralised by an acquaintance with those who pretended to be their benefactors, in communicating to them the glad tidings of salvation by Christ Jesus. Such is the testimony of the best writers on different parts of that continent, acquainted with different nations from North to South. It is given generally in the authors' own words, lest their meaning should be misrepresented, It must be confessed however that this is the fairest part of their character while at home and among friends: and it is a perfectly just one.

The chief and favorite object of their attention was originally hunting, in which sport they have been reduced to narrow limits, by the continual encroachments of the new settlers, and the building of towns amidst their originally wild and spacious woods. Large tracts yet remain open to them in many parts, but in general the remains of the old inhabitants have fallen by degrees into a state of partial cultivation, and have learned to depend more than formerly on the labour of their hands. In relation to their ancient sports we must speak of them as in times gone by. They are thus described.

Their haughty tempers will not condescend to labour: this they leave to the women. Their appearance is therefore solemn, except when they divert themselves with their principle amusements, dancing and gaming. In war, and when opposed to an enemy they are cruel and revengeful. They make war with unrelenting fury on the least unattoned affront. They kill and destroy their enemies without regret. To be a warrior is the highest object of their ambition. In their enmities they are bitter, and to avenge the blood of a kinsman they will travel hundreds of miles and cherish anger in their breasts for many years. They are anxious to carry home trophies of their success in war, but not so savage as that early nation of which we read in the 1 Samuel 18, 25 and 27, nor observing their hideous custom; they have from some source unknown adopted the less savage one referred to by David, in his holy anger against his enemies, whom he always designated, the enemies of God: they scalp the slain, as some Asiatics have done, contrary to the usage of all other savage tribes. David speaks of *the hoary scalp of his enemies.*

Before going to war, all that are able to walk and the old men borne by others, assemble in a grove or other place made sacred, and offer up prayer to the Great Spirit for success against their enemies. One of the old men addresses the assembly and recommends valour, and placing confidence in the giver of life. We are also told by Hunter, that a day seldom passes with an elderly Indian, or others esteemed wise and good, in which a blessing is not asked of Him and thanks rendered for his mercies. On occasion of an epidemic malady such meetings are also held, they are told that it is an infliction from the Great Spirit for some wilful offences, they are charged to repent, to ask for pardon and to amend their lives, all amusements cease and both private and public fasting is enjoined.

They usually attack with a hideous yell, so as to make

the woods to ring; the horror of which the ablest troops can scarcely withstand who have not expected such a reception. To women and children whom they take prisoners they are kind, and remarkable for the tenderness and delicacy with which they treat the former. To such prisoners as they, by certain rules, doom to death, they are insulting, cruel, and ferocious, and their women are ingenious in the science of tormenting them. But history will furnish us instances too numerous of cruelties among civilised Europeans, which neither savages nor even canibals can exceed: and there are instances on record of the behaviour of Englishmen towards those very people, cruel, revengeful and detestable in the extreme. If I do not attempt to justify the severities of the Indians, I must conceal from the eye of my readers facts which glare upon my sight in the history of my countrymen with the appalling look of a hyæna.

How much have men at all times, when they have laid aside the feelings of humanity and engaged in deadly warfare, how much have they regarded their fellow men with an eye of envy, of hatred, and of detestation! How much have they thought no cruelty too great to exercise towards them, let England in the times of persecution speak, let the history of protestantism and of catholicism almost equally declare, let Indians contending with Europeans, let Europeans invading the peaceful shores of the Atlantic and the burning sands of Africa also testify! —nay—let the sacred history vouch, when it writes of these very people under the conduct of a king and the instructions of the Priests of the Lord, that they did not then discover a better spirit than the forlorn wanderers in the wilds of America. See 2 Chron. 28. 5. and many other places!!

When a whole people change from a settled to a wandering state, especially if they remove from all connexion and intercourse with civilized countries, they must necessarily accommodate their actions to their pressing wants and necessities. Their usages will change with their circumstances. If before their emigration they had any knowledge of the arts and sciences, although this would enable them to exercise ingenuity and method in providing for their wants; yet, as they separated and colonized in different parts, this knowledge might gradually be lost, and little known of it but by tradition, except so far as should be kept alive by their actual wants.

It is well known that the people of Israel were never a scientific nor a mechanical people: the arts of life were carried on by their own households to supply their wants: they were their own millers, and weavers, and taylors, and carpenters. The Abbé Fleury, in his account of the Ancient Israelites, shews them to have been a people with comparatively little of civilised life known among them. They could scarcely be more polished by the event of the captivity; on the contrary their state would become worse; and during that period in which the Babylonian and Median Empires were striving for mastery, when the Persians spread their arms through all the east, and then too when the Macedonian crushed them all under his sceptre, very little progress could be made in the improvement of life, especially by a class of men so circumstanced as the captives were. In truth such was their condition, that they had every thing to [gain and little to lose, when the opportunity of escape presented itself, and a new and promising scene opened before them through the reports of travellers, perhaps some enterprising men of their own nation, and they heard of a Country, large, rich, and destitute of population, a still better Caanan, which they had only to seek and to possess.

The Indians are perfect republicans and will admit of no inequality except what arises from age or wisdom, for council or for war. But in war they observe a strict discipline and perfect subordination to their chief and to the officers who are chosen from the experience they have had in war, the management they have shewn in surprising an enemy or their wisdom in council. They are divided into tribes, and subject to a chief chosen from the wisest and bravest of them, and march under an ensign bearing the figure of the animal they have selected to distinguish them.

Every nation has its standard and every tribe its own badge or symbol. When they encamp, they cut the representation of their ensign on the trees, by which it is known who have been there. In treaties of peace or of friendly alliance their Sachem affixes the mark of his tribe, the figure of the animal, upon the treaty, as a corporation does its public seal. So among the Jews, the lion was the symbol of the tribe of Judah, the serpent of Dan, the wolf of Benjamin &c. But to no animals whatever do the Indians pay any religious respect.

Their leader is assisted by a council of old, wise and

beloved men.   Nothing is resolved upon but in this council where every one has an equal voice.   The chief is seated in the middle, and his council on each hand forming a semicircle, the manner in which the Jewish Sanhedrim sat before them.   The seriousness and extreme gravity which they observe, both old and young, in every affair of business was observed by Penn in his treaties with them, and by many others who had the opportunity of being present in their consultations.   They could not but admire the great reverence in which their aged and beloved men, as they call them, were held and the perfect submission with which their advice was received.   These men are generally poorer than the rest of the tribe: they usually give away the presents and the plunder which they obtain, so as to leave nothing for themselves. No kind of salary or stipend is annexed to any public office, to tempt the covetous or the sordid; and their authority resting on the esteem of the people, it ceases the moment that esteem is lost.   An old Mohawk Sachem, says one of their historians, in a poor blanket and a dirty shirt, may be seen issuing his orders, with an authority as arbitrary as a Roman Dictator.

Time is reckoned after the manner of the Hebrews. They distinguish the spring, summer, autumn and winter. The latter is called Korah by the Cherokees as by the Hebrews.   The years are numbered by one of its divisions for they have no name for a year.   Like the Israelites they count the year by months or moons.   They divide the day like them by the sun coming out, midday, and the sun being dead; they also speak of the midnight and

the cockcrowing. Their ecclesiastical year begins with
the new moon of the vernal equinox, according to mosaic
instruction. To the first appearance of every new moon
they pay great regard, and name the seasons from the
planting and ripening of the fruit. The green-eared
moon is the most sacred, when the first fruits are sanctified by being offered up.

When they travel they count their time according to
the ancient method by sleeps or more properly by nights,
making the evening and the morning the first day, and
so on.

The number and regular period of the Indian religious
feasts, as will be seen hereafter, is a fair historical proof
that they counted time and observed a weekly sabbath,
long after their arrival on the American Continent : for
the remark applies to all the nations. Before the seventy
years' captivity the Israelites, as stated by Prideaux, had
names for only two of their months, the one, the equinoc-
tial, Abid, signifying a green ear of corn; the other
Ethaniam, robust. By the first of these the Indians call
their passover, as an explicative, which the trading people
call, the Green-Corn Dance.

One of the Missionaries, being in the Creek nation on
a sabbath day, observed a great solemnity in the town and
a remarkable silence and retiredness of the red inhabitants.
Few of them were to be seen, their doors were shut and
the children kept within. He asked the meaning of it
and was answered, that being the white man's sabbath,
they kept it religiously sacred to the Great Spirit.

Boudinot being present himself on the Lord's Day at

the worship of seven different nations who happened to be at the seat of government, was pleased to see their orderly conduct. They were addressed with great energy by an old Sachem; and an Interpreter being present informed him that he had given an animated representation to his audience, of the love the Great Spirit had always manifested towards the Indians, more than to any other people, that they were in an especial manner under his government and immediate direction: that it was therefore the least return they could make for so much goodness, gratefully to acknowledge his favour, and be obedient to his laws, to do his will, and to avoid every thing that was evil and of course displeasing to him.

Just before the service began, he observed an Indian standing at a window, looking into a small field adjoining the house, where many white children were playing with the Indian children and making much noise. The Indian seemed displeased and expressed himself so, lamenting the sad state of those white children, whom he called, destitute orphans. He was asked "why he thought them orphans when they were not so." The Indian with earnestness replied—"Is not this the day on which you told me the white people worship the Great Spirit? and if so, surely these children, if they had parents or any persons to take care of them, would not be suffered to be out there, playing and making such a noise. No! No! they have lost their fathers and their mothers, and have no one to take care of them." With so much seriousness did he consider the business of a day devoted to religious worship.

Much might be said of their perfect subordination and

great skill in conducting war, which would throw considerable light upon the character of this people, but as this would lead us into too wide a field and embrace much which is not directly subservient to the object in view, it shall be passed over in silence. One subject however must be touched upon. When they determine upon war or hunting, they have preparatory religious ceremonies for purification, similar to those of the Israelites; evidently regarding the danger of losing their lives in these encounters, and the necessity of preparing for such awful event. Great however has been their secrecy in keeping their religious rites from the knowledge of the white people; and therefore mistakes have been made in the description given of those rites. The following account of them seems to be admitted by the best evidence that has been obtained.

"In case of an expectation of going to war, he who has the command fasts several days, besmeared with black and holding no conversation with any one: he invokes the Great Spirit by day and by night, and is careful to observe his dreams. The fast being over he assembles his friends and with a string of wampum in his hand he addresses them—"Brethren, the Great Spirit authorises my sentiments and inspires me with what I am to do. The blood of——is not wiped away, his body is not covered, and I will acquit myself of this duty towards him." Such is Charlevoix's account, that of M'Kenzie of another tribe, and at a later time, is this:

"If the tribes are called upon to go to war, the elders convene the people to obtain their opinion, they publish their intention to smoke in the sacred stem, a pipe, at a certain time. To this solemnity meditation and fasting are required as preparatory ceremonials. When assembled and the meeting is sanctified by smoking, in imitation perhaps of the incense of the Jews, the measures proposed are discussed. The chief then invites those who will follow him to smoke out of the sacred stem, as a sign of enrolment. A feast ensues with much seriousness and ceremony, after which the chief turning towards the east explains more fully the design of their meeting, and concludes with an acknowledgment for past mercies, and a prayer for the continuance of them from the master of life. He then sits down, and the whole company declare their approbation by uttering the word *Ho* in a hoarse guttural voice. The chief then goes round with the pipe from east to west to every one present, and the ceremony concludes."

These practices remind us of the instructions of the Jewish ritual, the purifications and sanctifying of individuals about to undertake important offices.

The Israelites humbled themselves and fasted in dust and ashes, the Indian besmears himself in token of humility.

Similar accounts are given by Adair and others, who state that, besides the fasting observed on these occasions they drink freely of a solution of bitter herbs which they call purifying, beloved physic, the effect of which is strongly purgative and offensive to the taste: and so observant are they of these old established customs, that they will not suffer any one, although engaged in the war with them, to enter their camp or have intercourse of any kind with them until he had undergone the purifying rites. This also savours of Hebrew manners. Deut. 23. 9. &c.

A friend just returned from Canada, brought with him a string of short pieces of an extremely bitter root which was given him as a matter of great favor by a chief with whom he was intimate. He described this root to possess great virtue. It is probably the casava, of which they make the bitter purifying liquor; the taste of it is extremely nauseous. Bitter herbs. Num. 9. 11.

The Hebrews carried to the wars with them an Ark or Chest. "And it came to pass when the Ark set forward, Moses said, Rise up Lord and let thine enemies be scattered and let them that hate thee flee before thee." And when it rested he said, "Return O Lord unto the many thousands of Israel." Num. 10. 35. "They presumed to go up unto the top of the hill, but the Ark of the covenant and Moses departed not from the camp." 14, 44. The Israelites were then smitten and discomfitted. See also 1 Chron. 15. 12.

In this Ark the ephod was kept, and by it David enquired of the Lord, 1 Sam 23. 9. The person who carried it was anointed with holy oil and was called, the anointed for the war. How the answer was obtained it is difficult for us to say: but we learn that before the temple was built this mode of asking council of God was frequent; there is no instance recorded of it during the time of the first temple. The Jews tell us, that during the tabernacle God spake by Urim and Thumim, under the first temple by the prophets, and under the second by a voice from the cloud.

The Indians have also an ark or chest which is carried with them to the wars of simple construction, only worthy of notice on account of the use that is made of it, about half the dimensions of the Jewish ark, carried by the leader himself or a beloved waiter who undergo a more severe purification than the rest, the one being Priest of war, the other helper to carry the ark while they are engaged in fighting. Consecrated vessels of antiquated forms are contained in the chest.

In the Percy Anecdotes is an account of an old Indian who was made prisoner when warring against another tribe. He assigned as the reason of his misfortune "that he had forfeited the protection of the divine power by some impurity, when carrying the holy ark of war against his devoted enemy." Which was a recognition of a God and his providence, and of the sanctity of the ark and the required purity of him that bore it.

It is never placed on the ground : where stones are plenty they heap them up and place it on them; but where there are no stones they have short logs of wood or a kind of tripod or three legged stool on which the ark and themselves may rest. Such was the pedestal on which the Jewish ark was placed. In the power and holiness of this ark they have a strong faith. It is deemed sacred; and no one, not even their own sanctified warriors, are permitted to touch it. No one may on any account med- dle with it except the war chieftain and his waiter, under the penalty of great evil. Nor would the most inveterate enemy among their own people touch it in the woods, through the same impression of its sanctity. Here may a striking comparison be made between these simple but superstitious people and the Hebrews before them—a comparison which will not hold with any other known nation of the earth: under this divine banner they carry on the wars.

This ark or chest appears to have degenerated with some of the smaller tribes into a sack. They carry with them in their war a kind of sack which contains their holy things, which they believe to have some secret virtue; and which is held in the same reverence as the ark of the other nations: this the conquerors would by no means touch if left on the field of battle.

The women are expected to take upon themselves all the household work—the men reserving themselves for war or for the chase. The women are treated with respect so long as they conduct themselves with propriety, and the greatest decorum is observed on all occasions towards them. Even to female prisoners no violence is ever offered: not the least indecency: their persons are sacred. But we are told on the authority of a Spanish Priest, that on the Oronoko if a woman is caught in the act of adultery, she is stoned to death before an assembly of the people, after the manner of the ancient Jews.

Another custom of the women must not be past over in silence. They oblige them in their lunar visitations to retire to a small hut at a distance from their dwelling houses, and there to remain, at the risk of their lives, a time that is thought sufficient. The general prevalence of this custom has been well established. See 15 ch. Lev:

A young woman, at the first change of frame, separates

herself from the rest in a distant hut and remains there for seven days or longer if necessary. Her food is brought to her by a person who may not touch her; nor may she touch her food with her hands. When the days are ended she baths herself in water, washes her clothes and cleanses the vessels she has made use of: the wooden ones she cleans with hot lye made with wood ashes, those of earth or iron she passes through the fire. She then returns to her father's house and is thought fit for marriage: but not before. Same chapter.

In some places a woman delivered of a child is separated in like manner for three moons or eighty-four days. By the levitical law a woman was to be separated and unclean forty days for a male child and eighty for a female. From no known law but this could the Indians have adopted a custom so strange, and especially since some of them observe a like distinction between the male and the female children. Leviticus 12. 2.

The ordinary character of the young women, in their first intercourses with Europeans, was that they were modest in their deportment and strictly virtuous: both young and old were highly offended at any indecent actions or even expressions: they were neat and clean. But there are two vices before which female modesty prostrates itself and is abandoned—drinking and gaming, the former of these has been the bane of the Indian women, as it has been the deadly plague of the Indian men.

While engaged in war, the Indians will not cohabit with their women; they religiously abstain from every kind of intercourse, even with their own wives, for the space of three days before they go to war, and also after their return home; because they are to sanctify themselves from all that has been wrong during the war. So Joshua commanded the Israelites, the night before they marched, to sanctify themselves by washing their clothes, avoiding all impurities and abstaining from all matrimonial intercourse: and so, Uriah, when called home by his licentious master, in order that he might, by intercourse with Bathsheba, hide the crime to which he had invited her, declined going into his house, and partaking of family delights while the ark of the Lord was in the camp and the war unfinished. And when the Indians return home victorious, they sing the triumphant song of Y. O. He. wah. ascribing the victory, as the Israelites did, not to their swords or arrows or to themselves, but to the Great Being.

When about to make peace, an embassy approaches the town, and a messenger is sent a head to inform the enemy of their pacific intentions. He carries in his hand a swan's wing painted with streaks of white clay, the emblem of a peaceful embassy. The next day they enter the beloved square, when their chief taking the lead is met by one of the old beloved men of the place. They approach in a bowing posture. The one asks, *Are you come as a friend in the name of the Great Spirit?* To which the other replies, *The Great Spirit is with me, I am come a friend in his name.* The beloved man then grasps the stranger with both his hands, around the wrist of his right hand which holds some green branches, then again about the elbow, then about the arm close to the shoulder as a near approach to the heart. He then waves an eagle's tail over the stranger's head, the pledge of good faith. This ceremony was observed between General Washington, and an embassy from the Creek nation in the year 1789. The common method of greeting each other is similar to the above. The host asks, *Are you a friend?* The guest replies. *I am come in the name of O. E. A. or Ye ho wah.*

These people are said to be extremely kind and affectionate to one another, always sharing among them whatever is given, and hospitable to strangers who visit them, giving them always the first piece of their victuals.

They are not only religiously attached to their tribe while living, but the bodies of the dead, especially their bones, are the objects of their solicitous care. The funeral rites which they observe shew that they have some notion of a future state of existence, and even of the rising of the body. They make a large round hole in which the body can be placed upright or upon its haunches, and placing the body in it, with the face towards the east, cover it over with what will support the earth above it and raise over it a little tumulus: the corpse is dressed in its best apparel, and near it are laid what was thought valuable and esteemed by the dead; if a warrior, his bows, arrows, hatchet or the like.

So free are these people from the spirit of covetousness, that to repress it in case of death, they burn all the little property an Indian has at the time of his death, or bury it with him in his grave.

Among the Indians of Canada when a person expires, the house is filled with mournful cries, friends are invited to lament with them, and these manifestations of grief are kept up as long as the expence can be borne. In some nations the relatives fast to the end of the funeral with tears and cries, and in others there are women whose business it is to undertake the office of weeping and wailing, and who go from house to house to relieve the family of the painful task—they sing, dance, and shed tears, always keeping time to their vocal strains. See Jeremiah 9. 17. "Consider ye and call for the mourning women, and send for cunning women that they may come, for a voice of wailing is heard." Some of these women have acquired the art of shedding tears at will, and they are much esteemed on these melancholy occasions. Those who have sought a resemblance between these Americans and the Hebrews, have not failed to notice in many different parts these cases of resemblance which support their opinion, finding them much resembling theirs. The Jews buried their dead in tombs hewn out of the rock, in which they were placed in an upright position, and often property valued by them was buried in their tombs.

The Southerns wash and anoint the corpse and take it out placing it opposite to the door, in a sitting posture: They then carry it several times round the house in which it is to be interred; for sometimes they bury it in the house and under the bed. In this procession the religious man, the Patriarch of the family goes before the corpse, saying in each round *Yah* then *Ho* which is sung out by all the company, he then shouts out *He* which is also sung by the rest, and all conclude by striking off with *Wah* in solemn chorus: which united sounds form the Tetragrammaton, or four lettered name of God, sacred among the Jews. Of which we must here observe, that the Hebrews are not permitted on any solemn occasion to utter this word; and that these Indians who certainly do use it, and in many parts are well known to use it, do so, not as an entire word, but by the sound of the letters apart and in the regular order which composed the sacred word. In the Choktaw nation and in several others they also distinctly sing *Hal-le-lu-yah,* intermixed with their lamentations. The account given of their funeral rites are much the same as those before mentioned.

The graves of the dead are so sacred among them that to profane them is the greatest act of hostility that can be committed against a nation; and they will not suffer a white man to be buried in the same ground with their own people; deeming it criminal, and believing that the spirits of the dead would haunt their houses and bring misfortunes on their families.

If any die at a distance from home and they are not pursued by an enemy, they place the corpse on a scaffold, secured from beasts and fowls of prey, and when the flesh is consumed and the bones dry they take them home and solemnly inter them.

The Indians on the Juniata and Susquehannah rivers, placed their dead on covered cribs made for the purpose, till the flesh consumed away. At the proper time they gathered the bones, scraped and washed them and then buried them with great solemnity. And there is a tribe called Nanticotes, who on their removal from an old to a new town, carry the bones of their ancestors with them, which was also known to prevail in some cases among the Canada Indians. Joshua 24. 32. 2. Sam. 21. 13.

Thus the Hebrews often gathered together the bones and deposited them in the tombs of their fathers. So Jacob charged his son to do after his death, and he buried him with his fathers in the cave in which his parents lay: and so Moses when he departed from Egypt took the bones of Joseph with him. The Jews buried near their cities and sometimes opposite their houses, implying a silent lesson of friendship and a lesson to live well. They buried families together, but strangers apart by themselves.

A respectable Clergyman, who preached to the Indians, was once present when news was brought to an aged woman of her son's sudden death by an accident. She retired to a distance and sat down on the ground, her female friends followed her and sat around her in a circle. They continued long in a melancholy silence, uttering only now and then a deep groan. All at once the mother put her hand to her mouth, and fell with her face to the ground, the others did the same, making melancholy and dismal yells and groanings. Thus they continued for some time with their hands on their mouths and their mouths in the dust. The men retired to a distance and went through the same ceremony. Need the reader be reminded of the relation which we have of Job and his friends. 21, 5; 29, 9; 40, 4. Micah 7, 16. Lam. 3, 29. Prov. 30. 32. and other places.

By the Mosaic law a surviving brother was commanded to take the widow to wife if she had no child, and raise up seed unto his brother. The design of which law was doubtless, to preserve the families entire, and that the inheritance of each might descend to the family. The children of the lawful wife had a right to the inheritance, and if the husband died before she had children, the brother, being the nearest relative was appointed to be the father of the heir at law. Ruth. 4, 10. Deut, 25, 5.

The Indian customs resemble this. A widow is bound by a strict law or custom to mourn the death of her husband for the space of three or four years. But if it be known that the elder brother of her deceased husband has lain with her, she is exempt from the law of mourning, has liberty to tie up her hair and anoint and paint herself; which she could not otherwise do without being treated as an adulteress.

Women have in no country nor at any period of time been treated with the regard and kindness they have experienced in Europe of late years. In eastern countries they were formerly bought, and wherever this mode of obtaining wives has prevailed their condition has been depressed; they have become the property and the slaves of the husbands. In this way were Rachel and Leah obtained: and in many parts of America the marriage contract is a purchase, if not of money, of an equivalent. The suitor devotes his service for a certain time to the parent of the maiden he courts, by hunting with him, cultivating his ground, forming his canoes or by other presents which are useful or rare. Their women are seldom prolific: excessive fatigue, together with the want and distress often incident upon savage life, the custom of suckling their children for many years, and it has been said the destroying of children when they exceed a convenient number, make the families small.

This mode of obtaining a wife which is found to prevail generally in the North, savours much of Israelitish manners; as does also their plan of divorce: for where a separation is desired, there is no wrangling about it, notice is given to the relations and the reasons assigned, little ceremony follows, no ill will is expressed and the divorce takes place. *Let him give her a bill of divorce.* This is an event by no means common. Deut. 24, 3.

In many places in which these Indians are settled, there are found among them places of refuge to which a criminal and even a captive may fly, and be safe from the avenger of blood if he can but enter it. Mr. Bartham, writes. "Here we arrived at the Apulachuela town in the Creek nation. This is esteemed the mother town sacred to peace: no captives are put to death or human blood spilt here." Adair states that altho' the Cherokees are exceedingly corrupted, still they observe the law of refuge so inviolably, that they allow their beloved town the privilege of protecting even a murderer, but they seldom allow him to return from it in safety.

The town of refuge called Choate, is situated on a large stream of the Missisippi. Here an Englishman was protected some years ago after having killed an Indian warrior in defence of his property. He told Adair that after some months stay in that town he proposed returning to his house which was in the neighbourhood: but the chiefs told him it would prove fatal to him. He was obliged to remain there until he had found means to satisfy the friends of the deceased by presents. In the upper country, there is also an old town, now reduced to a village, which is still a place of safety for those who kill others undesignedly, and in most other parts such spots still remain, in which no one was ever known to be put to death, though in their modern degeneracy they have sometimes driven persons out of them that they might be put to death elsewhere. Deut. 19, 2.

The Jewish law, Num. 35. 18. commanded that the murderer shall be put to death. The Avenger of blood shall slay the murderer; when he meeteth him, he shall slay him—but the same severe law provided a chance of escape. Cities of refuge were chosen in different and distant parts to which the murderer could fly and be secure. Numbers 35. 9. and following. So with the Indians, the nearest relative of a murdered man is bound to seek revenge and in general nothing but blood can atone for blood that was shed: nor is there any chance of a murderer shunning the fatal blow but by securing a retreat in one of their peaceful towns—where he is condemned to pass the remainder of his miserable life, to meditate on the evil he has committed and by repentance obtain the Almighty's pardon, while that of man is never vouchsafed to him.

" At the present day we can scarcely form an opinion of what these American Indians were when first discovered by the Europeans, They who see those people now, especially those who are near the new settlements and hold intercourse with the inhabitants, find them abandoned to all sorts of crime, mean, debased and grovelling, full of deceit and looking out for vengeance. By oppression, diseases and wars brought on them by the new comers, and especially by the free use of spirituous liquors, unknown to them in their pure state, of which they are immoderately fond, they have sadly degenerated in their moral character, and lost that sense of dignity and self importance which they formerly possessed. An old Charibbee, at an early day, thus addressed one of our people. "Our people are become almost as bad as yours. We are so much altered since you came among us that we hardly know ourselves; and we think it is owing to so melancholy a change that hurricanes are more frequent than formerly. It is an evil spirit that has done this, who has taken our best lands from us, and given us up to the dominion of Christians." Losing more and more of their old manners, they cannot at this time give any tolerable account of their religious rites and customs; although strongly attached to them as the express commands of the Great Spirit to their forefathers."

"The very ancient men who have witnessed the former glory and prosperity of their nation, or who have heard from the mouths of their ancestors, and especially from their beloved men, whose office it is to keep alive their traditions and laws and make them known to the rising generation, the former state of the country, the prowess of their warriors in old time and the peace and happiness of society, weep like infants when they speak of the fallen condition of the people. But this grief is not altogether without relief; for they have a prophecy of ancient origin and universal currency among them, that the man of

G

America, will, at a future day, regain his ancient ascendency, and expel the man of Europe from this western hemisphere. This flattering persuasion has enabled their prophets to arrest in some tribes the use of intoxicating liquors, and has given birth to attempts for a general confederacy of the Indians of North America."

Boudinot informs us he was present at a dinner given to some Indians in 1789 at New York, who had come there on a mission. Before dinner some of the Sachems with the Chief man were standing in the balcony looking at the city and harbour. They seemed dejected, especially the Chief. General Knox took notice of it and said, "Brother, what has happened to you, you look sad. Is there any thing to distress you.?" He made answer. "I'll tell you, brother. 1 have been looking at your beautiful city, the great water, your fine country, and see how happy you all are. But then I could not help thinking, that this fine Country and this great water was once ours. Our Ancestors lived here—they enjoyed it as their own in peace; it was the gift of the Great Spirit to them and to their children. At last the white people came here in a great canoe. They asked only to let them tie it to a tree, lest the waters should carry it away. We consented. They then said some of the people were sick, and they asked permission to land them and put them under the shade of the trees. The ice then came and they could not go away. Then they begged a piece of land to build wigwams for the winter; we granted it to them. They asked for some corn to keep them from starving; we kindly furnished it to them; they promising to go away when the ice was gone. When this happened we told them they must now go with their big canoes; but they pointed their big guns round their wigwams, and said they would stay there and we could not make them go away. Afterwards others came. They brought spirituous and intoxicating liquors with them, of which the Indians became very fond. They persuaded us to sell them some land. Finally they drove us back from time to time into the wilderness far from the water, and the fish, and the oysters: they have destroyed our game; our people have wasted away, and now we live miserable and wretched, while you are enjoying our fine and beautiful country. This makes me sorry, Brother, and I cannot help it."

They have above all things regretted the introduction of spirituous liquors among them, which with reason no doubt they regard as the greatest evil that has befallen them ; and the first and most decisive article in all their late treaties has been, that there shall not be any of it brought into their towns or sold to their people. The traders are allowed to carry enough for their own use, and what they do not consume must be thrown on the ground. Two young traders were met carrying forty kegs of Jamaica spirits into the Creek country by some of the natives, who immediately struck their tomahawks into every keg and let the liquor run out, without drinking a drop of it. This was a great instance of self denial; for it is said, their fondness for it is so great, that, had they indulged in tasting it, nothing could have prevented them from drinking the whole of it.

In the third report of the United Missionary Society it

is stated, "that the aged men, on hearing the children repeat the instructions given them in the school, were much pleased and said; "Now this is good talk. It resembles the talk which the old people used to make to us when we were little children; but alas! the wicked white men have rooted it out of our nation. We are glad the Great Spirit has sent these good Missionaries to bring it back to us again."

After some Missionaries had made known the object of their visit, the aged wife of one of their chiefs who was present made the following remark. "We have always understood, that at some time good people are to come, and teach us the right way; how do we know but these are those good people come to teach us?"

CHAPTER IV.

OF RELIGION AND RELIGIOUS RITES.

WHEN Mr. Penn had landed on the American shores and had held his first intercourse with the Natives of it, he was exceedingly struck with their appearance and manners. He found them very different from any people he had met with any where else, and thought them unlike any nation he had read of. He saw them in their state of native purity, undebased by slavery and uncontaminated with the vices of Europeans. In a letter to his friends in England he wrote, "I found them with countenances much like the Jewish race; and their children have so lively a resemblance of them, that a man would think himself in Duke's Place or Berry Street, in London, when he seeth them."

"They wore ear-rings and nose jewels; bracelets on their arms and legs, rings on their fingers, necklaces made of highly polished shells found in their rivers and on their coasts. The females tied up their hair behind, worked bands round their heads, and ornamented them with shells

G 3

and feathers, and wore strings of beads round several parts of their bodies. Round their mocasins they had shells and turkey spurs, to tinkle like little bells as they walked."

Of these things we read among the fantastic peculiarities of the Hebrew women in the days of their degeneracy, Isa. 3, 18. "In that day the Lord will take away the bravery of their tinkling ornaments about their feet, and their cauls and their round tires like the moon: the chains and the bracelets and the muflers: the bonnets and the ornaments of the legs, and the hand-bands, and the tablets, and the ear-rings: the rings and the nose jewels." "The common dress was a flannel garment or mantle ornamented on the upper edge by a narrow strip of fur, and at the lower edge by fringes or tassels. Over this, which reached below the knee, was worn a small cloak of the same materials, likewise fringed at the lower part;" which reminds us of the fringes and tassels worn by the Jews on their garments. They were then in the careful observance of certain religious feasts, which bore a remarkable likeness to those of the ancient Hebrews. Indeed many of the early visitors of this hitherto unknown country and most of the serious and intelligent part of the settlers, who paid attention to the people and to their customs, both Spaniards and Englishmen, made their remarks upon the general likeness they bore to the Jews; without unfortunately entering farther into the question, of the quarter from whence they sprang.

Speaking of religion, Father Charlevoix observes. "Nothing has undergone more sudden, frequent and surprising revolutions, than religion. When once men have abandoned the only true one, they soon loose sight of it, and find themselves entangled in such a labyrinth of incoherent errors, inconsistencies and contradictions, that there often remains not the smallest clue to lead us back to the truth. The Buccaniers of St. Domingo, who professed to be christians, but who had no intercourse except with one another, in less than thirty years, through the want of religious worship, instruction and an authority that might keep them to their duty, had lost all marks of christianity except baptism alone. Had those people continued only to the third generation, their grand-children would have been as void of christianity as the inhabitants of Terra-Australis, or New Guinea. They might, possibly, have preserved some ceremonies, the meaning and origin of which they could not explain."

The Israelites were carried captive about seven hundred years before the Christian era, and may have remained under the controul of their conquerors for two or three hundred years. We shall in a future chapter enquire about what period their escape from Media may have been accomplished; but, making every allowance that time and circumstances seem to require, it must have been nearly two thousand years after that escape, that these numerous and singular tribes were discovered on the American Continent. What surprising changes may not have taken place among them, or many parts of them, during that long term of years! Without government, without laws, without any head but the head of the family, or of a small associated tribe, or any will but that of the patriarchal chief; with an unlimited range over an immense continent, rich in natural Produce, and abounding in Game and

in wild Animals of various kinds; with more food at
their command than many years could consume, and the
prospect of their provision multiplying rather than dimi-
nishing; numberless will have been the modifications of
character which they assumed, and incalculable the distance—I mean in manners and in thoughts—from which
families and tribes will have receeded from one another.
And yet these wandering tribes of Indians, spreading
during the space of two thousand years, over an extent of
country ninety degrees in length with a proportionate
spread, have preserved so many essential parts of an
original plan of divine worship, and so many primitive
doctrines, as to satisfy enquirers, that they have descended from one family, and to point us with a sufficient
clearness to that family; while yet they have almost, and
in some parts wholly, forgotten their meaning and their
end.

It has been no uncommon thing for ignorant people to
charge them with being idolaters; the occasion of which
charge is well explained. Good men, from a want of the
knowledge of their language, and from an intimacy with
the most worthless of them, residing near the European
settlements, without making any allowance for situation
and circumstances, have given terrific accounts of these
children of nature. Some zealous and pious men, deeply
affected with a sense of what they considered their unhappy state, have gone into the woods to them, to preach the
Gospel, without a preparatory education for so important
an undertaking; without understanding their language
well, and knowing their customs, habits and prejudices.

Among some of these people it has been said there was a talk of many Gods; yet to this was added the declaration, that there is one great and good God, who is over all the rest: by the many gods may be meant the lesser spirits or angels, in which they all believe.

To persons so ignorant of what they ought first to have known, and trusting to a heathen interpreter who was unable to feel or express the nature of spiritual things, and having to deal with a jealous and artful people, rendered so by a suffering experience of more than a century, by imposition and oppression, what may we imagine would happen, but that they should be despised by the Indians, and then made a butt of to laugh at and to frighten. They have dressed themselves, for the sake of a frolic, in a terrific manner, and made frightful images, with extravagant emblems about them, to alarm the weak minds of the white people of whom they thought but lightly.

It is a well known fact that a preacher of this insignificant class went among them before the revolutionary war, and in his discourse began to tell them; "that there is a God who created all things; that it is exceedingly sinful and offensive to him, to get drunk, or lie or steal: which they should carefully avoid." They answered him. "Go about your business, you fool! Do not we know there is a God as well as you! Go to your own people and preach to them; for who gets drunk, and lies and steals more than you, white people?" Indeed, if the Indians form their ideas of us from the common traders and land speculators, and common people, with whom alone they associate, they will not run into a greater error than the

Europeans do, when they form their ideas of the character of Indians, from those that keep about the settlements and traffic with the frontier inhabitants.

Respectable as the character of Robertson is generally as a historian, he appears to have been deceived by the Spanish Writers to whom he trusted, though not implicitly. In his account of the Mexican religion there is much truth, mixed, as it appears from more recent investigation, with much error.

"Among the Mexicans religion was formed into a regular system, with a complete train of priests, temples, victims and festivals. From the genius of their religion we may form a just conclusion with respect to its influence on the character of the people. The aspect of superstition was with them gloomy and attrocious; its divinities clothed with terror and delighting in vengeance: they were exhibited under detestable forms which created horror. The figures of serpents, vipers, and other destructive animals decorated their temples: fear was the only principle which inspired their votaries; fasts, mortifications and penance were employed to appease the wrath of their Gods, and the Mexicans never approached their altars but with blood sprinkled upon them from their own bodies. Human sacrifices were deemed most acceptable; every captive in war was devoted as a victim, and sacrificed with rites no less solemn than cruel. The head and the heart were the portions consecrated to the Gods: the warriors who had made the prisoners, carried off the bodies to feast upon them with their friends. The Spirit of the Mexicans was therefore unfeeling, and the genius of their religion so far counteracted the influence of policy and the arts, that, notwithstanding their progress in both, their manners, instead of softening, became more fierce."

"In Peru, the whole system of civil policy is founded on religion. The Inca is not only a legislator but the messenger of heaven: his precepts are not received as the injunctions of a superior but as the mandates of a God: his race is held sacred and not intermixed with mean blood: he is the child of the Sun, and is deemed under the protection of the deity from whom he descended: his power is absolute, and all crimes committed against him are violations of heaven's decrees. The genius of religion was with the Peruvians quite opposite to that of the Mexicans. The Sun, the great source of light and joy and fertility in the creation, attracted their principal homage; the moon and stars, co-operating, were entitled to secondary honours." So the commands of Moses were those of God.

"There were no imaginary beings in Peru presiding over nature to occasion gloom; but real objects, mild and generous, made their religion gentle and kind. They offered to the sun part of those productions which his genial warmth had called forth from the bosom of the earth and reared to maturity. These people never stained their altars with human blood, but were formed to mildness by correcting all that is adverse to gentleness of character." Here is a thread of Persian theology woven into the theocracy of Israel. As their ancestors caught the Egyptian distemper, which burst out in the golden calf; so a tribe or family of the Israelites blended the Persian fire in their worship.

The Indians are filled with a spiritual pride, especially their chief and best men. They consider themselves under a theocracy, and that the Great Spirit whom they worship is in an especial manner their governor and head. They pay their worship, as Mr. Adair assures us, and he had the best opportunity of knowing, to the Great, Beneficent, Supreme, Holy Spirit of Fire, who resides above the clouds, and on earth with unpolluted, holy people. Some Spanish writers on their first arrival among them declared, that in Mexico they paid adoration to images or dead persons, or to the celestial luminaries or to evil Spirits; but Adair assures us, that the charge is totally false, although it may not have appeared to them altogether groundless.

Their religious ceremonies approach much nearer to the Mosaic than to Pagan institutions, but it is easy for observers to be deceived in these. Mistakes, and they very great, have arisen from the difficulty of a stranger obtaining correct information from a people who are jealous of the object of his enquiry, and extremely secret in performing their religious duties; and from the well known mischievous designs or avaricious views of strangers. A man who becomes a historian, if he be of a narrow mind and contracted view of things, delights in the marvellous, and makes up strange stories to answer private purposes or cover base designs: which has been fully exemplified in the false and base accounts which have been published by Spaniards of the inhabitants of Mexico.

Adair assures us, that from the experience of forty-years he can say, that none of the many nations from

Hudson's Bay to the Missisippi, have ever been known to attempt the formation of any image of the Great Spirit. Yet they are all a very religious people, and devout in their worship. They never attempt *to divine* from any thing but from dreams; which proceeds from a tradition, that their ancestors received knowledge of future events from heaven through this medium. Job 4. 12. 33. 15. and other places.

"The great temple at Mexico was a solid mass of earth in a square form, faced partly with stone. Its base on each side extended ninety feet, and decreased gradually as it advanced in height, terminating in a quadrangle of about thirty feet, where they placed a shrine of the Deity and two altars on which victims were sacrificed. All the other temples in New Spain resembled this." It is to be wished that Robertson who gives us this account had stated, what he meant by the shrine of the Deity. It may have been no other than the holy place, containing the holy things, which I have hereafter to describe, but which the Spaniards would convert into a proof of idolatry. On these points he seems to have had his thoughts completely perverted by the authorities in which he placed too much confidence. If his information was correct, and we are not authorised to say it was not, we are to regard this elevated plot of ground as a copy of the high places on which the inhabitants of Canaan worshipped their Gods; those of Dan and Bethel on which the calves of Rehoboam were placed; and others on which Baal—the Sun—was worshipped. But we are also to recollect, that the temple of Jerusalem stood on the highest ground, and, like the heathen

H

temples, was carried up as near the sky as could be.

Du Pratz was intimately acquainted with the guardians of the temple of a nation near the Missisippi, and, requesting to be informed of the nature of their worship, he was told, that they acknowledged a Supreme Being whom they call the Great Spirit, or the Spirit infinitely Great, or the Spirit by way of excellence. The guardian said, "the Great Spirit is so great and powerful, that in comparison of him, all other things are as nothing; he made all that we see, all that we can see, and all that we cannot see. He is so good that he cannot do ill to any one, even if he had a mind to do it. The Great Spirit made all things by his will; nevertheless, the little spirits, who are his servants, may by his orders have made many excellent things in the universe, which we admire; but God himself formed man by his own hands. The little spirits are free servants, always before him, and ready to execute his pleasure with an extreme diligence. The air is filled with other spirits, some good, some wicked; the latter have a chief who is more wicked than all the rest. The Great Spirit had found him so wicked, that he had bound him for ever, so that the other spirits of the air no longer did so much harm."

On being asked, how man was made? he answered. "That God kneaded some clay and made it into a little man; after examining it and finding it well formed, he blew on his work, and the little man had life, grew, acted, and walked." Of the woman he said, "probably she was made in the same manner as the man, but their ancient speech made no mention of any difference, only that the man was made first."

Hunter's Narrative was written, in 1823, under circumstances peculiarly striking. He was taken by the Indians when a child and brought up by them. He does not appear to have entertained any thought as to their origin or that of their religious opinions; but states many facts which clearly prove the point with us at issue. "It is certain that they all acknowledge one Supreme, all powerful and intelligent Being, the Great Spirit, the giver of life. They believe that he often held council and smoked with their red men in ancient times, and gave them laws; but that in consequence of their disobedience, he withdrew from them and abandoned them to the vexations of the bad spirit, who had been instrumental of all their degeneracy and sufferings." See page 25 and 26. "They believe him always present with them, and still loving those that pray to him and are thankful; they offer their devotions to him for preserving them and supplying their wants; and you then would witness the silent but deep impressive communication the native of the forest holds with his Creator."

Accounts very similar to these of the Northern Indians, are also given of the Araucanians and the inhabitants of Chili, whose history was written by Alonzo de Ericilla. They have the same traditions which prevail over North America, or very similar to them, they entertain the same views of God, and have the same religious customs.

In the South there are several instances of the theocratic form of government, in which despotism is concealed under the appearance of a gentle and patriarchal government. That of Zac, which comprised the kingdom of New

Grenada, was founded by a mysterious personage called Bochira, who, according to tradition lived in the temple of the Sun at Sogamoza two thousand years ago. The people are called Moscas. Sogamoza has been thought to be compounded of Sagan, the name of the Deputy high priest of Israel, which is also a well known Indian name for the deputy or waiter on their Priest, and Moses. Calmet tells us, that Moses was Sagan to Aaron, as he learns from the Rabbis. Hence this blind tradition of the Moscas may have confounded the names of the person and the place, or transferred that of the former to the latter, alluding in point of fact to their real lawgiver, Moses, two thousand years before some noted era.

They profess an opinion exactly similar to that of the Jews, that the Great Spirit is the head of their state, and has chosen them from all the rest of mankind as his elect and beloved people. This is a circumstance related not to a few, but to all who have had an intercourse with them, which would lead to the knowledge of it; nor can it well be accounted for, if they were not derived from the same stock as the Jews. Such is their religious pride, that they hold the white people in contempt, applying to them in their set speeches a word which signifies *nothing*. But they flatter themselves with the name, the beloved people, or holy people; and in their addresses they enlarge in boasting terms on the happiness of their country, and the special favour shewn it by God.

When any of the beloved people die, they soften the thoughts of death by saying, *he is gone to sleep with his beloved fore-fathers,* and have a proverbial expression among them, *the days appointed him are finished.* They affirm there is a fixed time and place, when and where every one must die, without the possibility of avoiding it. They also say, *such a one was weighed on the path, and made to be light;* ascribing life and death to God's unerring and particular providence.

"The Jews held the solemn four-lettered name of God in great reverence, and mentioned it only once a year when the high priest went into the holy place; and it is a striking fact ascertained by abundance of testimony, that the Indians utter loud the sound Yah at the beginning of their religious dances; they then sing y, y, y; ho, ho, ho; he he, repeating these sounds often, as if to retain the remembrance of the name, but never utter the whole word together; at the sound of Yah, which so nearly resembles the word Jah, the abstract of Jehovah, they fall into a bowing posture." Whence can have come this veneration for certain sounds, their frequent and regular repetition on religious occasions, and their care not to unite them in one sound so as to utter the whole word? Such an extraordinary resemblance to a Jewish feeling and a Jewish reverence can scarcely have been an accidental occurrence in the life of those tribes.

Charlevoix, speaking of the northerns, observes "that the greater part of their feasts, their songs, and their dances, appear to have had rise in religion, and still preserve some traces of it. There is a great resemblance between them and the people of God. At some of their meals they do not use knives, and are careful not to break any bones of the beast they eat; and never eat the part which lies under the lower joint of the thigh, but always throw it away." Other persons have said they throw it into the fire. "They have been often heard to utter distinctly the word Hallelujah in singing; and at the return of their hunting party they make a feast of which nothing must be left, but all consumed, or entirely disposed of before the next morning; as in the passover of the Israelites; and if any family cannot accomplish the prescribed command, they call in the assistance of their neighbours; as was practised in Canaan when a family was not large enough to consume the paschal lamb."

" The American Indians, especially the Cherokees and Choktaws, have in their places of worship, as they call them, the beloved squares, a very humble resemblance of the Cherubim which overshadowed the mercy-seat. Adair saw in one of these squares, two white painted eagles, carved out of poplar wood, with the wings stretched out, standing in a corner five feet from the ground, close to the red and white imperial seats, and within were painted with a white clay the figure of a man, with buffalo's horns, expressive of power, and that of a panther, which is the nearest of the animals of America to a lion. Compare Ex. 37. 9. Ezekiel chap. 10. Each of the Cherubims, according to the prophet, had the head and face of a man, the likeness of an eagle about the shoulders, with expanded wings, the neck, mane and breast of a lion, and the feet of an ox: See Ezekiel, 1. 5. In these squares they dance on the winter nights, singing Hallelujah; also yo, he, wah: but never discover any signs of adoration of these figures." When the Israelites

encamped we ·learn of them, that they were usually arranged into four divisions, under four different standards,
namely, a man, an eagle, a lion and an ox, which four
emblematic figures, whatever they may mean, were found
roughly drawn in this and other similar temples.

The terms of their language direct to the character of
their religious feelings. The southerns call God by a
name which signifies greatness, purity and goodness; *the
great, beloved, holy cause:* persons and places set apart,
are called sanctified; which epithet is also applied to their
priest or holy man, calling him, *the great, holy, beloved,
sanctified man of the holy one.* The most sacred appella-
tive they have for God is that already mentioned, yo, he,
wah, which they do not utter in common speech. Of the
time and place of uttering it they are very particular,
and it is always spoken in distinct syllables, and with a
solemn air.

They have among them an order of men answering to
both prophet and priest. With some their language calls
them cunning men, and prescient of futurity, but generally men resembling the holy fire. Their tradition reports of them, that in former times they were possessed of
an extraordinary divine spirit, by which they foretold
things future, and controuled the common course of nature; and they believe that, by the aid of the same divine
spirit or fire, they can still effect the same. These perhaps,
were the lineal descendants of the tribe of Levi.

A similar account of the prophets of the Delaware
nation, was given by Mr. Beatty about sixty years ago.
" They consulted them upon occasion of great sickness,

mortality, or other extraordinary occurrences; as the Jews of old enquired of the prophets. These people are called, beloved men, and their pontifical office descends by inheritance to the eldest."

I scarcely think it necessary to enter here into a minute description of the dress of the priests, which it will be supposed, in their rude and distressed condition, cannot have retained the richness of the ancient priesthood : it is however astonishing to see how much, in their humble style, it corresponds with that of the Jewish priesthood. There is with them a long and a solemn ceremony once a year for making the supposed holy fire, and offering a yearly atonement for sin, when the priest is clothed in a white garment, resembling the Ephod, made of a finely dressed deer-skin : it is a waistcoat without sleeves : his shoes and other garments are white and new, and worn only on that occasion: —he puts on a breast-plate, made of a white conch-shell, with white buttons on the outside, in imitation, we will venture to say, of the precious stones of urim and thummim. Round his temples is a wreath of swan's feathers, or a piece of swan-skin doubled, so as that only the snowy down may appear; corresponding in a humble degree with the plate of gold of the Jewish High priest; and on his head a tuft of white feathers : on his mocasins are fastened a number of blunted turkey-cock spurs, as the Jewish High priest wore bells on his coat of blue.

In every town or tribe is a High priest, and others of inferior rank. The oldest presides in spiritual things : he maintains great influence among his people, and the great council never determine on any point of importance without his advice. The people firmly believe, that they have communion with invisible spirits, who have some share in the government of human affairs, and also of the elements. Their incense is the smoke of tobacco, which they puff about on some occasions, and blow towards the sun; and they reckon their time by the new moon, of which they are great observers, and rejoice at its coming as the Hebrews did before them.

There is an odd story among them, which may be conceived to have had its birth from their knowledge of the blazing stones of the urim and thummim. It is of a transparent stone of supposed great power to bring down rain, when put into a basin of water, agreeably to a divine virtue impressed on one of them in times of old. This stone would suffer injury if it were seen by any common person, and if seen by foreigners would lose all its divine power.

" They have also a most holy place, into which none but the priest can enter. It is partitioned off by a mud wall, and in it are deposited their consecrated vessels. To approach this sacred spot would occasion danger to themselves, and general injury to the tribe. The great public square, or beloved place, stands alone in the centre and highest part of the town. It has four square or cubical buildings, enclosing a spot large in proportion to the size of the town: one of these is the council-house—another a dark building, a secluded place, designed for a sanctuary or temple, into which it is death for any but the High priest to enter; in which are deposited, the sacred things, the physic pot, rattles, chaplets, eagle's tail, calumet, or sacred stem, a sort of pipe, the pipe of peace, &c."

Mr. Bartram was once present in a town when the people were fasting, taking medicine to purge thoroughly the system, and praying the Great Spirit to avert from them a sickness which had long afflicted them. They fasted seven or eight days, taking no food but a meagre gruel, made of corn, flour and water, and drinking a black drink which acted as an emetic. Deut. 16. a fast of seven days.

In short, their ceremonies of religion are much after the mosaic plan, and have scarcely any resemblance to Pagan institutions, while they are utter strangers to all the gestures practised by the pagans in their religious rites.

To the above remarks, which apply chiefly to the North American Indians, it is desirable to add the remarks of early writers on the state and customs of those of Mexico and of South America. These writers have been chiefly Spaniards, who cared little about the religious feelings of the natives, and appear to have done all in their power to have them regarded as idolaters, cannibals, offering human sacrifices, barbarous and premeditated murderers. There were indeed some happy exceptions among those writers.

From these persons we learn, that they offered to the sun and earth a small quantity of every kind of meat and drink before they tasted it themselves. This was the evening sacrifice already explained. Montezùma shut himself up and continued for the space of eight days in fasting and prayer when the Spaniards arrived ; and to blacken his character they have added without sufficient authority, that he offered up, human victims in sacrifice to his God. These prayers and fastings were doubtless the same as those of the Northern Indians, to sanctify himself and gain favour and council from the Deity. At Mexico was found a temple, with a priest, called the minister of holy things, together with the hearth or altar, the continual fire, the holy ark, &c.

Bertram gives a description of a Southern Indian temple, composed of a square of small buildings; " here they held their councils; a part was shut up, being esteemed holy, into which the priest alone entered, and where the sacred things were deposited. At this temple, he says, the males assemble three times in a year, at the feast of ripe fruits, at the hunting feast, about the time of the ancient pentecost, and at the great feast of expiation, at the time of ripe corn. When one dies, the Indians, like the Hebrews, wash and anoint the body."

Of the Peruvians, Acosta relates, "that they held an extraordinary feast, for which they prepared by fasting two days, not accompanying with their wives, or eating salt meat or garlic or drinking *chicca* during that time. They assembled in a place, which neither strangers nor any beasts were allowed to enter, afterwards they danced and feasted." Here is the Northern's festival of Atonement for Sin. He adds.

"The Charibbeans at a triennial feast divided the women and children from the men; the latter, shut up in a house, sang, *he, he, he,* while the others answered by repeating the same : they danced to the sound of rattles, the beloved man being dressed in pontifical garments." They have also a kind of feast of love or friendship similar to tha already described. The Mexicans have also the feast when the corn is ripe, on which occasion every one brings to the temple a handful with a drink made of the same."

Lact, in his description of South America, assures us, "that he often heard the Indians repeat the word *hallelujah*." and Malvenda states " that the natives of St. Michael had tomb-stones with ancient hebrew characters upon them, as these. *Why is God gone away ; and, he is dead. God knows.*"

The Mexicans have also the tradition of a deluge, in which one man was saved with his family and different animals ; and a Portuguese historian in his history of Brazil, says, " America has been wholly peopled by the Carthagenians and Israelites. As to the last, nothing but circumcision is wanting to constitute a perfect resemblance between them and the Brazilians."

Other authorities similar to these might be quoted from the early Spanish and Portuguese writers. What has been given is sufficient to answer the end designed in selecting them.

There has recently appeared in this country, The Secret Report on America, by Ulloa and Juan, written according to the instructions of the Secretary of State, and presented to Ferdinand the 6th. One of the most important points to which the authors of this report directed their attention, was to redeem from calumny the character of the native Indians, whose supposed incapacity had been made the pretext of so much injustice and cruelty. The country is stated by them " to be covered with the ruins of magnificent works of public utility, erected by them, which the Spaniards thought them incapable of executing. Solid paved roads four hundred leagues in length, aqueducts which brought water a hundred and twenty leagues, temples and palaces of a most splendid character, were the monuments of an empire only four hundred years old when Pizarro visited Peru, and found a people eminent in the arts which adorn a highly advanced state of civilization : and yet this people, because they have sunk under the bigotry and oppression of their plunderers, are farther libelled with the charge of imbecility and incapacity. The truth is, that nothing has tended to depress the people and weaken them more than the measures which the Spaniards adopted to make them christians."

A young Clergyman of Plymouth who went out with Captain Mends in 1825, in the Ship Blanche, took considerable pains to examine the antiquities which still remain in abundance all along the Peruvian coast for many leagues, running parellel with the sea and the mountains. There are still, not only the remains of stupendous works of great antiquity : but there are also extensive ruins of temples and fortifications made of burnt brick. He dug into the cemetaries, an immense line of burial places, to all appearance the receptacles of many generations, and disinterred some bodies, which were in a state of perfect preservation, and are now lying in the British Museum. The bodies were dry, consisting of bone and skin carefully wrapped up in cotton cloth. In the tombs in which these bodies were laid, small earthen vessels were found in the rough form of a bottle with a handle or handles, the bottom round, and having a mouth-piece, generally in the handle, out of which the contents of the vessel might be taken. Some of these have the form of a fish, some of a bird, and some are plain: a few are double made in two distinct parts, united at the side by a brace three or four inches long, with two orifices terminating in one, intended perhaps for the tomb in which two persons united in life were interred. These vessels were stopped at the mouth, and contained a small quantity of fine dust, the remains of a food which the survivors deposited in the grave of their friends, to supply their immediate want in the event of a revival.

The tomb of a Casique, which is distinguishable by its being situated in the centre of the burial place of his tribe, was opened by some of the crew of the Cambridge in the same year; and, besides the body of the chief, the skeletons of twelve men were found, and on their skulls were clearly distinguishable fractures, as from an axe or tomahawk; who are said to have been sacrificed at his death in order to be buried with him, that on his rising again he might not be unaccompanied by a proper retinue. In the graves are also found such instruments or articles as correspond with the character of the deceased, and would be proper for them to resume on their rising again. Thus, in that of the warrior were instruments of war, the spear, the axe and the arrow; in another's and he probably addicted to the sea, a very small canoe, or a fishing rod in miniature; in the woman's grave was discovered a rough kind of distaff, with thread still on it in a perfect state of preservation, also wooden needles, and the like. The earthen vessels, or bottles, as they may be called, are of different sizes, and may contain a quarter of a pint or a half pint, —there are two large enough to hold about two quarts, which we will suppose were designed for the Casique and his attendants. On some of them is the serpent, distinctly formed with the tail in its mouth, the Egyptian and Babylonian emblem of Eternity; on others the rough figure of a bird, perhaps the Apis of Egypt, not unknown in Chaldea. There are other characters also, which may be emblematical, or merely fanciful according to the whim of the potter.

These kinds of things have been shewn in Europe as proofs of the idolatrous disposition of the natives of America;—but, as well might the uncouth images which disadorn our old cathedrals, and were the sports of monkish days, in which the cleverest fellow was he who could frame the oddest image,—as for instance; the Devil on the Witch's back who is looking over Lincoln—as well might these be adduced as indications of the idol worship of the dark ages, as many of those articles which are handed about by our Missionaries, and other credulous persons, to awaken the zeal of public meetings and obtain money for the conversion of the Heathen.

The natives have for the most part forsaken the spot where these venerable remains and the ashes of their fore-fathers still are seen, and retired backwards towards and amongst the long range of the Cordilleras; leaving the Coast in the hands of their conquerors, and now inhabited by a motley race made up of Europeans, Indians and Africans, mixed and mixed again in an indiscriminate succession. They are however very numerous in their back settlements, and remain pure and uncontaminated by what they may well regard as base and defiled blood.

There is a striking similarity in the opinions which

have been discovered amongst the scattered nations and tribes of that Continent, in reference to the object of their worship. Speaking of the Deity, they call him, the Spirit, the Great Spirit, and the Spirit of fire; some indiscriminately: but the Peruvians carry their symbol worship still farther. Their Incas are Children of the Sun: the first of them descended from the Sun to give them Laws: their temples are temples of the Sun. Yet we are not to suppose that the Sun itself was their God. They directed their attention to that bright luminary, as the ancient Persians and Chaldeans did, because it is the direct dwelling Place of the Great Spirit—as we say, Heaven is God's throne. But they certainly have formed no images of their God, nor did they plant Groves around their temples, as the Canaanites and the Druids were used to do: so often referred to in Scripture.

In almost all other parts of America the dead were placed on their haunches, the face towards the East, that on revival they may hail the rising Sun: but it is remarkable that in Peru, which is bounded on the East by an uninterrupted range of lofty mountains, and where the Sun is not seen till it has risen high in the heavens, the dead are always found in the same position with their faces towards the West—that they may behold his setting, since his rising is not within their view.

Of the Antiquities of Mexico and the Missisippi, I shall speak in a future chapter.

CHAPTER V.

IT will be proper to give a particular account of the festivals of the American Indians; for in all ages and in all generations religion has been connected with festivals, and the indulgence of the appetite has formed a part of the gratitude to be paid to the giver of all blessing. Those who have written on the feasts of the Indians, specify five that bear strong characteristic marks, by which the philosophical enquirer may be assisted in forming his opinion of the ancient stock from whence they sprang. These are. The feast of first fruits, the hunters' feast, the feast of harvest, a daily sacrifice, and a feast of love. Of all habits those of religion are the most powerful, and keep the fastest hold.

Mr. Penn, who acquired his knowledge of this people from his own observation, informed his friends in England in the year 1683, that "their worship consisted of two parts—sacrifice and cantico: the first is for their first fruits. The first fat buck they kill goes to the fire, where

1 3

it is all burned with a doleful chaunt of the priest, and with such fervency and labour of body that he sweats to a foam. The other is the cantico, performed by round dances, words, songs and shouts, and drumming on a board." At one of the feasts Mr. Penn was present: it consisted of twenty bucks with hot cakes made of new corn, of both wheat and beans, in a square form, wrapped in leaves and baked in the ashes: when these were eaten they fell to dancing. Every visitor takes with him a present in their money, which is made of the bone of a fish, the black is as gold, the white as silver; they call it wampum. He also remarks "that they reckon by moons, they offer their first fruits, they have a kind of feast of tabernacles, they are said to lay their altars upon twelve stones, they mourn a year, they have a separation of women"; and other things which do not occur in the present day.

From Mr. Adair we have the following abstract of a feast which may be called, the feast of first fruits.

"On the day appointed, as soon as the spring produce comes in, while the sanctified new fruits are dressing, six old beloved women come to the temple or sacred wigwam of worship, and dance the beloved dance with joyful hearts. They observe a solemn procession as they enter the holy ground, carrying in one hand a bundle of small branches of green trees; where they are joined by six old men, adorned with white feathers, having green boughs in the other hand. They ate dressed in shewy ornaments. The oldest man begins the dance, going round the holy fire in solemn silence: in the next circle he invokes *yah*, after the usual manner, on a bass key and with a strong accent : in another circle he sings *ho, ho,* which is repeated by all the religious procession, till they finish the circle. Then in another round, they repeat, *he, he,* in regular notes, keeping time in the dance ; another circle is made in like manner, repeating *wah, wah.* A little while after this is finished they begin again, going fresh rounds singing, *hal-hal-le-le-lu-lu-yah-yah,* in like manner, and frequently the whole train strike up, *halelu, hallelu, halleluyah, halleluyah,* with earnestness, fervour and joy, each striking the ground with right and left foot alternately, strongly and well timed. Then a kind of hollow sounding drum joins the sacred choir, on which the old women chaunt forth their grateful praises to the Great Spirit, redoubling their steps in imitation of the beloved men at their head." This is similar to the dances of the Hebrews, some of whose dance-songs had no doubt the word *halleluyah* at the beginning or ending. These degenerate people, losing their ancient language, and with it the words of these festive songs, have still retained the chorus sound, as that which made the deepest impression and was known by all; and it is well attested, that all the inhabitants of the extensive regions of North and South America, have and retain these very expressive sounds, and repeat them distinctly in their religious acclamations. Deut. ch. 26. especially verse 11.

On other religious occasions they have been distinctly heard to sing *ale-yo, ale-yo,* the divine name expressive of omnipotence : also, *he-wah, he-wah,* intimating the soul, or eternity, derived from *yo-he-wah.* These words of their religious dances are never repeated at any other time;

which has contributed to the loss of their meaning, for it is thought they do not now understand either the literal or the spiritual meaning of what they sing, any further than by allusion to the name and the praise of the Great Spirit.

"In these circuitous dances they frequently sing on a bass key, *aluhe, aluhe, aluwah, aluwah*; also *shilu-yo, shilu-he, shilu-wah* and *shilu-hah*. These they transpose in several ways, with the same notes. They continue their hymns of joy for the space of about fifteen minutes and then they break up. As they degenerate they are said to lengthen the dance and shorten the fast and purificacation; and so exceedingly are they known to have changed within the last seventy or eighty years, that if they continue to decline from the manners of their ances- tors, there will not ere long be a possibility of recognising them, but by their dialects and war customs: which also will alter. After the dance is over they drink plentifully of bitter liquids to cleanse their sinful bodies; and then go to some convenient water, and there, according to the cere- monial law of the Hebrews, they wash away their sins. They then return with joy in solemn procession, singing songs of praise, till they enter the sacred square, to eat the new fruits which are brought to the outside of it by the beloved women. They observe the greatest decorum in these solemnities, and give the name *kanaha* to any who violate them. There is a subdivided tribe on the North part of Pensylvania called Kanaa or Kanai, a sound much like Canaan."

Accounts very similar to this are given by other writers.

Dr. Beatty states thus what he saw: "Before they make use of any of their first fruits, twelve old men meet and provide a deer and some new fruits. They are divided into twelve parts, the old men hold up the venison and pray with their faces to the east, acknowledging the bounty of heaven towards them. It is then eaten, after which they freely enjoy the fruits of the earth. On the evening of the same day they have another feast which looks something like the passover; when a large quantity of venison is provided with other things, and distributed to all the guests, of which they eat freely; and if any is left it is thrown into the fire and burned, for none of it must remain till sun-rise on the next day, nor must a bone of the venison be broken." Num. 9. 12. Deut. 16. 4.

The feast of Passover was observed by the Hebrews not in their own houses, but in a sacred spot, which the Lord should choose to place his name in, Deut. 16. 6; and in America we find these people observing their feast in the sacred place of worship, or in the beloved Square.

I shall now proceed to describe the Hunter's Feast. This is thought to resemble the feast of Pentecost. The reader may judge. After their return from a hunting expedition, during which they leave their families for a certain space of time, longer or shorter as may be required, they have a feast of gratitude.

Dr. Beatty says "that once in a year, some of the tribes beyond the Ohio choose twelve men, who go out and provide twelve deer; others have ten men and ten deer.—these numbers of twelve and ten deserve attention —each of them cuts a sapling, and stripping off the bark they make a tent by striking the ends in the ground and bending them close at the top, covering them with blankets. Each man chuses a stone, which they make hot and place together in the form of an altar within the tent, on which they burn the inside fat of the deer. See Num. 18. 17. Lev. 8. 25. While making this offering, the men within cry out, *we pray or praise,* they without answer, *we hear:* then from the tent the sound proceeds, *ho-hah,* loud and long. When the fat is consumed, they burn tobacco cut fine on the same stones, by way of incense. Of this altar, so like to the jewish altar, it is to be remarked, that no tool may be used in shaping the stones of which it is built, they are taken rough, and no instrument of any kind employed in building them up. Deut. 27. 5 and 6.

The Southern Indians have a similar custom; if they have been successful on any occasion and returned safe, they offer a sacrifice of gratitude : but if they have lost their men, they imagine they have been impure and mourn for the sin which occasioned their loss.

Like other ill-informed and superstitious people, the poor Indians imagine that their sins are the procuring cause of all their evils : thus did the friends of Job ; and that the Divinity in the ark will always bless the more religious party with success. This is with them a governing sentiment, and the reason of mortifying themselves in the severest manner while they are at war, living scantily, lest by luxury their hearts should grow evil and give them occasion to mourn. *Thou shalt afflict thyself.*

Beatty, who went at an early period into the Delaware nation, was present at a great meeting on a consultation

for going to war with a neighbouring nation. "They killed a buck and roasted it, as a kind of sacrifice, on an
altar formed of twelve stones, upon which stones they
would not suffer any tool or instrument to be used. The
whole of this animal was afterwards eaten by them excepting the middle joint of the thigh." Genesis 32. 25
and 32.

"The Muskohgee Indians sacrifice a piece of every
deer they kill at their hunting camps or near home. If
the latter, they dip their middle finger in the broth and
sprinkle it over their domestic tombs, to preserve them
from the power of evil spirits; according to their mytho-
logy of those beings. This custom seems to have a view
to the sprinkling with blood: no other semblance offers
itself in the history of antiquity." Lev. 8. 15 and 19.

The Feast of Harvest and Day of Expiation for Sin.

The Indians formerly observed this solemn feast and
fast, and the offering of the first fruits of harvest, at the
beginning of the first new moon in which their corn became full-eared: but for many years past, they have
regulated it by the forwardness or backwardness of their
harvest.

According to Charlevoix, "the harvest is in common
with the Natchez, on the Missisippi. The Chief fixes the
day for beginning the festival, which lasts three days,
spent in sports and feasting. Every family brings something obtained by hunting, fishing or other means, as
maize, beans and melons. The Chief presides and on the
last day addresses the company in a set speech, exhorting
them to the punctual performance of their respective du-

ties, to a high veneration for the Spirit which resides in the temple, and to a careful instruction of their children. Of the first produce a part is brought to the temple; and also of all presents made to their nation, which are distributed according to the pleasure of the Chief. But the offerings every new moon are for the use of the keepers of the temple. This feast is preceded by a fast of two nights and a day. This feast was kept by the Hebrews in the month Tizri, the first month of the civil year, answering to September and October: it took place previous to the great day of expiation, the tenth of the month. About this time the Indian corn is full-eared and fit to eat, and nearly about the same time their feast of harvest is observed." Lev. 1 and 2 ch. Priest's Portion. Num. 18.

To meet the letter of the divine precept, the Jews on the eve of the Passover festival, which was to be eaten with bitter herbs, instituted a rigorous search through every part of their houses, not only removing all leavened bread, but sweeping every part clean that no crumb should be left. Leaven may be regarded as the emblem of sin, because it proceeds from corruption. On the next day they offered to God a handful of barley which, the high priest, seasoning with oil and frankincense, presented to the Lord: then was offered the lamb, a whole burnt-offering, together with fine flour mingled with oil; also a drink offering of wine: and they were forbidden to eat either bread, or parched corn, or green ears, until the offering was made to God. Lev. 23. 14.

"When the feast is over, the holy place is carefully cleaned out, the old hearth or altar is dug up, the temple is swept, so that not the smallest crumbs should remain to defile it, and a preparation is made for obtaining the holy fire. In the mean time the women are busy at home in cleaning their houses and putting out their fires. All being ready for the sacred solemnity, the remains of the feast are carried to the outside of the square, every thing is removed, even the vessels and utensils of every sort which have been used during the past year. The warriors and old men are then called by proclamation to come into the beloved square, and keep the fast: the women and children are kept apart, according to their law: all living creatures are forbidden to enter except those who have been called, and the fast is then kept until the rising of the second Sun; no temptation whatever prevailing with men in health to take food during that time—while they are drinking plentifully of a decoction of the button-snake root, to make them vomit and cleanse their sinful bodies —but children and weak persons are allowed to eat after the Sun has gone down. May not the snake-root used by those in the temple, and the bitter green tobacco which is taken by the women and those who by reason of defilement have not been admitted to the square, point to the bitter herbs of the family of Israel? Proclamation is then made to enquire, whether the old fire is every where put out; for that the holy fire will be brought from the temple. The beloved man and his attendant go to the holy place, and taking a piece of dry wood, cut a hole in it, but not so deep as to go through; he then sharpens another piece, and placing it in the hole, he drills it briskly between his knees till it begins to smoke; or by rubbing

K

two pieces together for about a quarter of an hour, he ob-
tains by friction the hidden fire ; which they believe proceeds from the holy spirit of fire. This they cherish with
fine chips, till it bursts into a flame. The fire is then
brought out from the holy place and put upon the altar;
at which they exceedingly rejoice, supposing all their past
crimes except murder to be atoned for. An offering is
then made of some new fruits rubbed with bear's oil on the
altar, Lev. 8, 10, to the bountiful spirit of fire, all sinners
are called on to appear, the high priest gives injunctions
to the people, presses upon them the necessity of a careful
observance of the ancient law, and directs that the holy
fire should be laid outside the consecrated ground for the
use of the houses, which are often some miles apart." This
custom very much resembles one which was observed by
the ancient Persians as well as by the Jews.

" After the ceremony is ended the priest orders them to
paint themselves and follow him. They appear rubbed over
with white clay, and form a slow procession to a running
stream, singing *halleluyah* or *yo-he-wah*, into which they all
plunge, men, women and children. Thus being purified
and their sins washed away, they think themselves out of
the reach of temporal evil on the ground of past conduct."

Similar statements have been made by other persons, of
the same feast held by the Southern Indians; and that
they collect together all old and filthy and unclean things,
and cast them into a large fire, take medicine, fast for
three days, extinguish all their fires, abstain from the
gratification of every appetite, proclaim a general amnesty,
and recal malefactors to their houses ; then by friction

they obtain new fire, with the pure flame of which every habitation is supplied. They then sing, dance and rejoice, keeping feast for three days. They also burn the fat of the inwards in the fire.

The Feast of the Daily Sacrifice was offered by the Hebrews every morning and evening. It consisted of a lamb, and was all burnt to ashes excepting the skin and the entrails. The Indians seem to observe a humble imitation of it. Some persons who have been adopted by them and lived in their families, tell us, "that they observe a daily sacrifice, both at home and in the woods, with new killed venison. They draw it before it is dressed several times through the fire and smoke by way of sacrifice, and to consume the blood, which to eat would be an abomination to them: the melt or a large piece of the fat of the first they kill is consigned to the fire; and within their houses a small piece of the fattest of the meat is thrown into the fire before they begin to eat." Lev. 8. 25.

A feast of Love, to renew old friendships, has been also observed among them, in which the people eat, drink, and walk together with arms entwined: the young men and women dance in circles from evening till morning, to gladden their hearts and unite them before *y, o, he, wah. &c.*

Mr. Boudinot informs us, that he was present at a dance given by the Seneca Indians, six or seven nations united, in return for a hospitable entertainment given them by the English Governor, of which we have the following description. "After the company had assembled in a large room, the oldest Sachem and a beloved man entered with a kind of drum, on which the former beat time; upon which between twenty and thirty Indians came in, wrapped in their blankets. These made a solemn and slow procession round the room, keeping a profound silence, the Sachem's drum directing their movement. At the second round they began to sing on a bass key, *y, y, y,* till they completed the circle, dancing to the sound of the drum in a serious manner. On the third round, their ardour increased, they danced to a quicker step, and sang *he, he, he,* so as to become warm, to perspire and to loosen the blankets. On the fourth round they sang *ho, ho, ho,* with greater earnestness, and, dancing with more violence, their heat increased, and they cast away the blankets; which caused some confusion. The last round put them into a mere frenzy; they twisted themselves about, wreathed like snakes, made the antic gestures of a parcel of monkies, singing all the while with great violence *wah, wah, wah.* They kept perfect time to the music, each round occupying ten to fifteen minutes. They then withdrew in Indian file. In a short time a great bustle was heard, when they re-entered and danced one round—then a second, singing in a lively manner, *hal, hal, hal,* till the round was finished, then another to the word *le, le, le,* and a third to *lu, lu, lu,* dancing naked with all their might, having thrown the blankets off again: during the fifth round was sung the syllable, *yah, yah, yah.* Then, all joining in a lively chorus, they sang *hal-le-lu-yah,* dwelling on each syllable with a long breathing and in the most pleasing manner."

Here could be no deception nor mistake. Mr. B. was near them: their pronunciation was guttural and sonorous, but distinct and clear.

The Indian Priests or Prophets or beloved men are always initiated by anointing. Some time ago the Chickesaws set apart for holy purposes some of their old men. They first obliged them to sweat themselves for the space of three days and nights in a small hut, made for the purpose at a distance from the town: they ate nothing but green tobacco leaves and drank the button-snake-wood tea, to cleanse their bodies and prepare them to serve in the holy office. After which their priestly garments were put on them with the other ornaments, and then bear's oil was poured upon their heads. Like the Jews, even in the coldest weather, they observe religious ablutions, and frequently anoint themselves with oil. See Lev. 8. 6. for the consecration of Aaron and his sons.

They never prostrate themselves nor bow their bodies to each other, by way of salute or homage, except when they make peace with strangers, who come in the name of *yah:* they then bow with religious solemnity: and in the dances when they sing hymns addressed to *y, o, he, wah.* It is also said that they will not eat of the Mexican hog nor the sea-cow nor the turtle, but hold them in abhorrence: neither will they eat the eel, nor many animals and birds which they deem impure, as eagles, ravens, crows, bats, buzzards, owls, and others.

It has been remarked of the Indians throughout America from North to South, and from East to West, that they are all, men, women and children, addicted in an extraordinary degree to the use of strong liquors. I fear it may be said to be a propensity equally strong in all uncivilized nations, when it can be obtained. Many persons have thought, that it is still stronger in the American Indians than in any other people, and in this striking fact they have seen the fulfilment of prophecy. Moses foretold that the people should *walk in the stubbornness of their own hearts, to add drunkenness to thirst:* and in the 28th of Isaiah we read of *the drunkards of Ephraim* from the first to the eighth verse; in which their devotedness to strong drink is expressed, and the base effects of it. Now the Jews have never been observed to be given to drunkenness, but rather the contrary. Amidst temptation they have been generally sober and regular: but these descendants of Israel, if such they are, have been inveigled and destroyed through their devotedness to strong drink more than through any other causes. Their enemies have employed this seducing foe, first to weaken and entrap, and then to pilfer and murder them. Among the vices which European society has brought on them, this has been the most predominant, enfeebling and destroying both mind and body. Long have they seen the evil, and many of the best of them have struggled hard against it; but to little purpose; for it seems not possible for them to withstand this all-conquering enemy. They make laws against the use and even the introduction of spirituous liquors among them, and with great firmness often destroy large quantities which are brought in by the traders by stealth. But if once the lip touches the forbidden drink, all the reasoning and authority of their beloved men will not prevent their drinking as long as a drop remains; and they generally are so overcome by it as to be like mad foaming bears. Of this vice they were

free, and did not even know it, before the landing of christians on their shores; but it is strange now to tell, how
all their nations, and almost every individual of them, are
infatuated with the love of strong drink. By its means
they have been made to quarrel with and kill one another; and it has brought them to the practice of vices,
which, in the eyes of their beloved men, are a disgrace
and a degradation to them.

*　　*　　*　　*　　*　　*　　*　　*　　*

In the Monthly Magazine for April 1828, is the following paragraph.

"An opinion has long prevailed, that Columbus introduced into Europe from America the disease at present
known under the appellation of syphilis. This question,
which has been agitated during three Centuries, has been
at length set at rest by the researches of Dr. Thienne, a
Physician of Vicenza, who has satisfactorily proved the
ravages of this disease long before the birth of Columbus.
His investigations have led to some curious remarks;
inasmuch as he has established a sort of analogy and identity between the elephantiasis, the leprosy, the venereal
infection of Canada, the sibbens of Scotland, the radzyge
of Norway, the saws of Africa, the pan of America, the
malady of schertieno in the Tyrol, &c."

Now if there be a real correspondence between these
virulent diseases, which are found on different spots
and in varied climates, the Doctor may have erred in
imagining he has discovered that species of the disease in

question in the annals of a period prior to Columbus. And the generally prevailing opinion may be true—that it was brought into Europe from America, corroborated by his own remarks of its similarity with other prevailing complaints. It is well known that the Israelitish nation were in old times much subject to the leprosy; which disorder may have assumed a new character upon a new soil, under the influence of a new and very different manner of living, and with habits so very unlike those which prevailed among them when inhabiting the well cultivated regions of Asia. If so awful a visitation had been experienced under similar circumstances in Greece and in Rome, it must be regarded as a most extraordinary fact, that it is not described, nor distinctly alluded to, by the numerous writers of those nations : and had it been known in Europe previous to the voyage of Columbus, it would surely have been clearly defined and the mode of cure pointed out by our own Surgeons.

The disease called Brenning or Burning, which prevailed in England in the fourteenth and fifteenth Centuries, appears to have had a great resemblance to the Syphilis; but as that was a period when the leprosy was common throughout Europe, this complaint was probably a peculiar, being a local, branch of it. For Leprosy see Lev. chap. 13 and 14.

CHAPTER VI.

OF THE LANGUAGE OF THE INDIANS.

THIS is the most difficult part of the subject before us; for, were we inclined to yield to the evidence already produced, to shew the many points of resemblance between the ancient Hebrews and the Indian tribes, we can scarcely expect to find enough of the old language remaining to furnish a fresh evidence of their kin. The Indian languages have never been reduced to any certainty by written characters: it has never even been thought to form a grammar by which it shall be taught to their children. Masters and Professors they have none of any kind. Traditions only have been conveyed down from father to son ; and these, during a long course of years, and in the mouths of hundreds and thousands of instructors, have so changed, that they assume different faces on different spots, by some are altogether lost, and by many are upheld in a rough and careless manner, without any knowledge of their origin and of their rational or spiritual design. Of art and science they are comparatively ignorant : no monuments of antiquity are standing memorials with the present race : oppressed on every side, driven from home to home, as circumstances have varied, and homes been abandoned, language has undergone many changes ; and not a little variety will have arisen as new families sprang up and new tribes were formed, from the simple circumstance of the construction of the organs of speech ; which even among ourselves occasions the same words to be so differently pronounced, that a foreigner, understanding them when proceeding from one mouth, is often at a loss when they are uttered by another. Putting idioms out of the question, and new words coined to express new things, the very names of things in common use will be expressed by many inflexions of the voice, so as to become in the ears of a stranger different words. Take for example the sound of many of our vocables uttered in the streets of London, in the villages of Yorkshire and among the mines of Cornwall, and many of our familiar expressions. We do not ourselves often know what our own countrymen say, on a spot where every thing is done that can be done to preserve the purity of our language : of purity indeed we must be silent when we speak of the use of words in the mouths of the unlettered of our Island.

Of the Indian languages, which are numerous, and to an European ear very unlike, it has been observed, that they are copious and expressive, more so than might be expected with a people whose ideas must be few in comparison with those of civilized nations. They have neither cases nor declensions ; few or no prepositions ; but like some of the ancient languages abounding in affixes and prefixes: the words are the same in both numbers.

It has been said that no language known in Europe, except the Hebrew, is destitute of prepositions, as separate and specific words. They have no comparative or superlative degree, but express them as the Hebrews do by terms dignified and honourable. Thus the Cedars of Lebanon, famed for their loftiness and grandeur, are in the Hebrew the Cedars of God, and a mighty wind is a wind of God. So with the Indians, the superlative is formed by one of the letters of the divine name being added to the word. Their public speeches are adorned with strong metaphors in correct language and often with allegory. An example or two may be acceptable to the reader.

About the year 1684 the Governor of New York sent an agent, on a dispute likely to arise with the French, who behaved in a haughty manner before the Indians. One of the chiefs answered him in a strain of simple eloquence, in which he said among other things, "I have two arms: I extend the one to Montreal, there to support the tree of peace, and the other towards Corlaer *(the Governor of New York)* who has long been my brother. Ononthis *(of Canada)* has been these ten years my father. But neither the one nor the other is my master. He who made the world gave me this land I possess. I am free, I respect them both, but no man has a right to command me, and none ought to take amiss my endeavouring all I can, that this land should not be troubled. I can no longer delay repairing to my father, who has taken the pains to come to my very gate, and has no terms to propose but what are honourable."

At a meeting held with General Washington in 1790, a chief called Cornplant, who had always shewn great friendship for the white people delivered an impressive speech, of which this is an extract.

"Father, when your army entered the territory of the six nations, we called you the town-destroyer; and to this day when your name is heard, our women look behind them and turn pale; our children cling close to the necks of their mothers: but our councellors and warriors being men, cannot be afraid: their hearts are grieved by the fear of the women and children, and desire that it may be buried so deep as to be heard of no more. Father, we will not conceal from you, that the Great Spirit has preserved Cornplant from the hands of his own nation. You told us, say they, that a line drawn from Pennsylvania to Lake Ontario would mark our land for ever on the east; and a line running from Beaver Creek to Pennsylvania would mark it on the west. But we see that it is not so. For first one and then another comes and takes it away by order of that people, who you told us would secure it to us for ever. Cornplant is silent, for he has nothing to answer. When the sun goes down Cornplant opens his heart before the Great Spirit, and earlier than the sun appears again upon the hills; he gives thanks for his protection during the night, for he feels, that among men become desperate by the injuries they sustain, it is God only that can preserve him. Cornplant loves peace: all he had in store he has given to those who have been robbed by your people, lest they should plunder the innocent to repay themselves."

What follows is a sentence of a speech of an Indian Chief to his companions, in a war oration. He told them, "he feelingly knew that their guns were burning in their hands; their tomahawks were thirsty to drink the blood of their enemies, and their trusty arrows were impatient to be on the wing; and lest delay should burn their hearts any longer, he gave them the cool refreshing word, '*join the holy ark*,' and away to cut off the devoted enemy."

A speech made by Logan, a famous chief, about the year 1775, cannot perhaps be excelled by any of the highly celebrated examples of Grecian, Roman or British eloquence. In revenge for a murder committed by some unknown Indians, a party of the Americans fired on a canoe loaded with women and children, all of whom happened to belong to the family of Logan, who had been long a staunch friend of the white people and then at perfect peace with them. A war immediately ensued, and after much blood-shed peace was restored. A treaty was proposed, but Logan disdainfully refused to be reckoned among the suppliants for peace.

"I appeal," said he, "to any white man to say, if he ever entered Logan's cabin hungry, and he gave him not meat —if he ever came cold and naked, and Logan clothed him not. During the last long and bloody war, Logan remained idle in his cabin, an advocate for peace. Such was his love for the white men, that my countrymen pointed as they passed and said, *Logan is the friend of white men*. I had thought to have lived with you, but for the injuries of one man. Colonel——— the last spring, in cold blood and unprovoked, murdered all the relations of Logan, not

L

sparing even my women and children. There runs not a drop of his blood in the veins of any living creature. This called on me for revenge. I have sought it. I have killed many. I have fully glutted my vengeance. For my country, I rejoice at the beams of peace. But do not harbour a thought that mine is the joy of fear. Logan never felt fear. He will not turn on his heel to save his life. Who is there to mourn for Logan? No, not one."

Energetic and eloquent as is this address, under the painful impressions in which it was given, let the reader remember how extremely difficult it is to obtain a translation of such an example of oratory that conveys the spirit of the original: few languages will admit of it, and, the simpler and less redundant the language in which it was delivered, the more difficult it must be to retain the genuine character in the diffuse terms of modern tongues.

Mr. Adair, who had the best opportunities of becoming acquainted with the idioms of their language by a residence of forty years among them, has taken great pains to shew the similarity of the Hebrew to the Indian languages, both in their roots and general construction; and gives reason to believe that many of their words are even to this day pure Hebrew, notwithstanding the danger it has run of perpetual change, so as to render the preservation of even a part of it little less than miraculous.

It is well known that the original Hebrew, which was spoken by the Jews before the captivity in Babylon, was a language very different from that which was afterwards known to the people of Jerusalem, and is now known to the descendants of that people. Our learned men even now declare that the old language of the Jews is lost; that it was more properly a Phenician or Chaldaic idiom, and that it was during the captivity of no more than seventy years that they adopted an idiom essentially different, that of Babylon, together with its character. What shall we then say, if only a similarity can be shown, and a fair comparison can be established, between the terms of the natives of this wilderness, and those of the stock from whence we maintain that they are sprung?

Father Charlevoix was a man of learning and of respectable abilities: he paid more attention to the Indian languages than perhaps any one before him or since, and he had greater opportunities. These are his remarks.

"The Algonquin and Huron languages have between them that of almost all the savage nations of Canada: whoever should well understand both, might travel without an interpreter more than fifteen hundred leagues of country, and make himself understood by a hundred different nations, who have each its peculiar tongue. The Algonquin has an extent of twelve hundred leagues, and they say that it prevails to a much wider extent."

"The Huron language has a copiousness, an energy and a sublimity perhaps not to be found in any of the finest languages we know of; and they, whose native tongue it is, though now but a handful of men, have such an elevation of soul, as agrees much better with the majesty of their language, than with the state to which they are reduced. Some have fancied they found in it a similarity with the Hebrew; others have thought it had the same origin as the Greek." "The Algonquin language has not so much force as the Huron, but has more sweetness and elegance. Both have a richness of expression, a variety of turns, a propriety of terms, a regularity which astonishes : but what is more surprising is, that among these barbarians, who never study to speak well, and who never had the use of writing, there is never introduced a bad word, an improper term or a vicious construction. Their children preserve the purity of their language in their common conversation. The manner in which they animate all they say, leaves no room to doubt of their comprehending all the worth of their expressions and all the beauty of their language."

We must not detract in any respect from the virtue and the discernment of this excellent man, in his attempts to serve a nation of human beings whom he regarded as infinitely beneath himself in spiritual knowledge. They were his children, he had adopted them in Christ Jesus, and he loved them as such; and perhaps gave them more credit for their regular advantages than others would have done. Yet he could not be altogether deceived, and his judicious remarks are of the utmost importance in giving us a just view of the inhabitants of the back settlements, from the boreal regions of Canada to the mild shores of the Mexican Gulf.

Dr. Edwards, Son of President Edwards, a man of great learning, who was intimately associated with the Indians from the age of six years, and understood their language as well as his mother tongue, and a Mr. Elliot who was called, the Indian Apostle, and translated the Bible into the Mohegan language, have given us much information respecting it. "For the pronouns, which are common in other languages, they use letters or syllables placed at the beginning and the end of words. In this particular the structure of their language coincides with that of the Hebrew in an instance in which the Hebrew is said to differ from all the languages of Europe, ancient and modern; with this difference, that the latter place affixes at the end of words, whereas the former to express the singular number prefix the letter or syllable, but in the plural, place it at the end: They also change and transpose the vowel to express the possessive pronouns." Dr. Edwards has pointed out a number of instances in which the analogy between these two languages is striking: and he tells us, that the Mohegan dialect, which is that of which he writes, is spoken over a very large extent of country, and is to others a sort of mother tongue: it seems to be the same as others call the Algonquin, from another tribe using the same dialect.

A tribe has been thought to be discovered among them corresponding with the tribe of Levi. The Mohawks, once very numerous, were held by all the other tribes in great reverence, and even in fear; so that they fled before them, made neither war nor peace without their advice, and paid them an annual tribute. The Mohawks were the correctors of what was done amiss by the other tribes.

Now it is worthy of an incidental remark, that the name of this nation greatly resembles the Hebrew word which signifies a law-giver, or interpreter of the law, Meichokek. Gen. 49. 10. Law-giver between his feet.

To enlarge upon the subject of language would not

accord with the limits I have prescribed to myself in the size and price of this volume. I can only subjoin the remark—that there are a number of verbs and of nouns which are nearly or altogether alike in the two languages, notwithstanding the change which time, and the difference in the organs of speech, and the fancies of an untaught people must of necessity have occasioned. The pronunciation of this people is so guttural as to make even the Hebrew words appear different to those who are looking for them : their language consists of a multitude of monosyllables added together; every property or circumstance of a thing being noted by an additional syllable. A very natural way for an untaught people to express their meaning. Making reasonable allowances for these and other causes of change in names and in pronunciation, it is next to marvellous that so great an affinity between them should still subsist; and most of all, that in their religious associations, these nations, who have changed their manner of expression in the common intercourses of life, have preserved those sacred words and use them with the same precaution, which have distinguished the people of God from the days of Moses to the present time.

Souard, in his Melanges de Litterature, speaking of the Indians of Guiana observes, on the authority of a learned Jew, Isaac Nasic, residing at Surinam, "that their language is soft and agreeable to the ear, abounding in vowels and synonimes: that all the substantives are Hebrew : that the word expressive of the soul means breath, that they have the same word as in Hebrew to denominate God, which means master or lord."

CHAPTER VII.

ON THE INDIAN TRADITIONS.

THE Indians do not possess the advantage of conveying the knowledge of old times down to posterity by means of writing: this can be preserved only by tradition: therefore young men have been selected by the judgment of the old ones, of merit and good character, to be the channels through which the manners and customs of their ancestors shall be made known to distant generations. Without specifying the sources whence these traditions were received, because that would make it necessary to write more than is necessary for information, and many of them have come from different and distant tribes, I shall state the chief and most important of these traditions.

They hold it as a general and a certain fact, that all the tribes came into that country from the same quarter, in ages very remote, from a far distant country by the way of the North-west, that all the people were of one colour, and in process of time moved eastward and southward to their present settlements. Those of Mexico state, that their fathers were settled in another place before they came to their present abode, that they wandered eighty years in obedience to the command of the Great Spirit in quest of new lands under particular directions given to them, and having obeyed the divine directions they were guided to Mexico.

The Southerns say, that their ancestors lived beyond a great river. That nine parts of their nation passed over the river, but the others refused and staid behind: that when they lived far west they had a king who left two sons: that one of them, with a number of the people travelled a great way for many years till they came to the Delaware river, and settled there. They have it handed down from their ancestors, that the book which the white people have was once theirs: while they had it they prospered: but the white people bought it of them and learned many things from it; whilst the Indians offended the Great Spirit, lost their credit and suffered exceedingly from the neighbouring nations: that the Great Spirit took pity upon them and directed them to this country: on their way they came to a great river, which they could not pass, but God dried up the waters and they passed over dry shod: that their fathers were possessed of an extraordinary divine Spirit by which they foretold future things and controuled the course of nature, whilst they obeyed the sacred laws: but that this power had left them.

M'Kensie writes—they have a tradition, that they came from another country inhabited by wicked people, and had traversed a great lake which was narrow, shallow and full of islands, where they had suffered great hardships and much misery, it being always winter, with ice and deep snows: at a place they called the Copper-mine River, where they made the first land, the ground was covered with copper, over which a body of earth had since been collected to the depth of a man: their ancestors had gone on till their feet were worn out with walking and their throats with eating: they spake of a deluge, when the waters spread over the earth, except the highest mountain on the top of which they were preserved: they also believe in a future judgment. He remarks, " whether circumcision be practised among them I cannot pretend to say, but the appearance of it was general among those I saw." On this subject we have still more explicit information from several quarters; that it was generally practised long ago, but that the young men, not knowing the use of it or why it was practised, made a mock of it, brought it into disrepute and so it fell generally out of use: that the people went formerly to build a high place, and while they were building it they lost their language and could not understand one another, while one called for a stick a stone was brought to him; and from that time they began to talk different languages: that the first woman came from Heaven and had twins, and that the elder killed the younger. The Southern Indians mention, that when they left their native land, they brought with them a sanctified rod, by order of the oracle, which they fixed every night in the ground, and were to remove from place to place on this continent, towards the rising sun, till it budded in one night's time, that they obeyed the sacred oracle and the miracle at last took place when they arrived at the Missisippi.

That in the beginning the heavenly inhabitants, as they called them, frequently visited the people and talked with them, and gave directions how to pray and how to appease the Great Being when he was offended; to offer sacrifice burn tobacco, &c.

That there are two great beings that rule and govern the universe, who are at war with each other. The one, Maneto, is all kindness and love; and the other Matche-maneto delights in doing mischief: some say they are equal in power; others that Maneto is the first great cause, and therefore must be all powerful and supreme and ought to be adored, whereas the other should be rejected and despised.

When Cortes advanced to attack the capital of Mexico, its King Montezuma told him, "that it was an established tradition among them, that their ancestors came originally from a remote region and conquered the provinces now subject to his dominion, that after they were settled their great captain who conducted the colony returned to his own country, promising that at some future period his descendants should visit them, assume the government and reform their constitution and laws: that, from what he had seen of Cortes and his companions, he was convinced that they were the persons whose appearance the Mexicans' traditions and prophecy taught them to expect, that accordingly he received them not as strangers but as relations of the same blood, and desired them to consider themselves as masters of his dominions, and that he and his subjects should comply with their will." There is not any way of accounting for the strange fatuity which seized upon this unhappy monarch, but by ascribing it to the confused recollection of the authority of Moses and the promise he gave of one rising up after him, like unto himself, whom the people should obey. In one thing however he was inflexible. They could not by all their tantalizing promises and cruel tortures draw him from the worship of the Great Spirit to adopt the rites which they prescribed.

Many of Robertson's remarks on the manners and practices of the Mexicans and the Peruvians are evidently taken from Spanish historians, and are pointedly denied by the Colonists, who have taken great pains of late years to make themselves acquainted with those people.

The Rev. Jabez Hyde, New York County, remarks in a letter to the Author of The View of the Hebrews, dated 1825. "I have long been of opinion that the natives of this country are the Outcasts of Israel. Most of the particulars you mention I know to be facts. After reading the Star in the West I paid more attention to the subject. In the year 18 a general religious excitement commenced among the Senecas. They attempted to understand and reform their old religion. The wise men assembled who were best acquainted with their mysteries; they had no idea of the meaning of their feasts, and dances, nor the words they made use of in them. They consented to take the book which the white men call, the Word of God, to throw light on their path. This was the commencement of Christianity among them, which brought in two who had officiated as high priests: they have given me an unreserved account of all they know of their ancient religion, and were desirous of learning whether any things in our scriptures were similar to their customs. They are firmly persuaded that they are the people of God, but have lost their way and are bewildered in darkness." Mr. Hyde then gives a statement of their customs and religious observances, similar to what has been stated already.

The entire discontinuance of the Sabbath among these tribes may be regarded as an argument against the hypothesis which the forementioned facts go to establish. It may be said; "If they have preserved the sacred words and continued the ancient festivals of the people of Israel, how is it they have lost their Sabbath day, the most peculiar of all the characteristics of God's people. Habit would surely confirm them so strongly in the observance of that day, that they could not possibly forget it; and if some extraordinary revolution, like that of the days of terror in France, should obliterate the day of rest from the almanack, because it had been a religious festival, we should see it revived in some other form; like the decade of the French Revolution."

There does seem much force in this remark: for we are so completely the creatures of habit, that even a slight deviation from our ordinary routine cannot be effected, without disturbing our peace and producing unpleasant sensations: much less can our religious associations be interrupted without offering a severe violence to our feelings. But I am led to remark on this apparently strong objection, that it is evident, from the denunciations of the prophet, that this custom of keeping a Sabbath day, which was a practice entirely unknown to the Heathen nations, had lost its force with the Hebrews long before these people arrived on the Western continent, supposing that they ever did arrive there. From the 17th ch. of Jeremiah, we learn, that the inhabitants of Judah had broken the fourth commandment in so notorious a manner as to call down the indignation of the Almighty against them. verse 21. "Thus saith the Lord: Take heed to yourselves and bear no burden of the Sabbath day, neither do ye any work; but hallow ye the Sabbath day, as I commanded your fathers. But they obeyed not, neither inclined their ear, but made their neck stiff, that they might not hear nor receive instruction."

Now if this was the character of the inhabitants of Jerusalem, who did retain a respect for the ordinances of Moses, and never plunged into Idolatry as the Israelites did; it is no great demand made upon our faith to believe, that these latter had been prevailed on, long before they were driven out from their happy land, to give up the observance of a Sabbath day. The idolatrous women with whom they had so generally associated, the people of the land whose abominations they had adopted, the example of their Kings and Queens who forsook God, would above all things separate them from a custom which belonged to them as a distinct race; and in the attachment they formed to the pagan worship, to the Calves of Rehoboam, and the Baals and Ashtaroths of the land, they would, as a matter of course, follow the observance of days and times to which those people were devoted. In former times public festivals were connected with religion; and

M

when whole societies of people were converted to Christianity, the ancient festivals were generally preserved, and, with a slight alteration, were made to answer for the Christian worship. The Israelites would probably retain their festivals, being that part of their original institutions which well suited the carnal appetite, and they would still have a regard to these in their new places of abode. With annual festivities no system of religion, not even the Christian, is offended; while therefore they retained theirs, there would be no peculiar inducement for them to resume the interruption of a day of rest. From traditions still preserved, however, there is good reason to believe, that a Sabbath was observed by some of the tribes after their arrival in America: but, when it ceased, and why, we have no means of ascertaining. It is well known, that the rite of circumcision was in use among some of the tribes even at a comparatively late period of time, but was given up, according to their traditions, by the young men, because they thought it an unnecessary and even a cruel custom, and did not know for what reason their ancestors had appointed it. The Sabbath may have been abandoned under a similar persuasion, that there was no necessity for its observance.

Thus those ancient customs which afforded a peculiar gratification retained a feeble and half expiring life, while others from which no pleasure was acquired were by degrees suffered to sink into oblivion.

CHAPTER VIII.

ON THE PASSAGE FROM CONTINENT TO CONTINENT.

THESE traditions of the aboriginal nations of America which have been found in different parts of it, and some, indeed most of them in many parts, with such shades of difference as may be expected to exist, may now be connected with the discoveries which have been made at a later period of that part of the Northern ocean which lies between the Western shore of America and the opposite coast of Kampschatka; and a farther corroboration will present itself of the important fact it is the object of these pages to establish.

Kampschatka is a large peninsula on the North-eastern part of Asia, a mountainous country, with a cold and frozen climate. The Islands, in this narrow sea which divides it from America, are now numerous; they are subject to continual earthquakes, discover evident marks of repeated volcanos, and abound in sulphur: so that it may well be imagined, that in the course of many Centuries great changes have taken place in that part of the sea, and that a chain of islands may have run across, forming an easy communication from continent to continent at all times, and especially in the winter season, when the land and sea would form one continued track of solid ice. The strait is often filled with ice at the present time, so as to afford a free passage ; and when the water is free, it is very shallow: so that it is no great stretch of probability to suppose, that two thousand years ago the two continents were joined, though little known to each other by reason of the severity of the climate that must have been endured in passing from the one to the other, and the inhospitality of the soil in the North-eastern part of Asia: an abundance of unoccupied ground still lying open to the tribes and families that were wandering about what we now call Siberia.

The Northern parts of the two continents where they approach have been found to abound with the same kinds of animals, bears, wolves, foxes, hares, deer, roebuck, elk and the like, nor was it until the number of these had been greatly diminished in the European continent, that the hunters crossed the narrow strait to sport on the American land, in which their numbers were immensely great and they were so tame that they were easily taken .

We are also informed by Robertson, that "when Peter the Great determined on exploring the North-east part of his empire and the seas lying thereabout, a tradition was found to exist, that a communication had been held with the opposite coast: in those provinces an opinion prevailed, that there are countries of great extent and fertility at no great distance from them."

Du Pratz, who wrote in the year 1720, informs us, that he met with a very intelligent Indian who had travelled to the North-west, through a pressing curiosity to see the land from whence his forefathers came, but found it cut off therefrom by the sea to his great disappointment. He there heard of a very old man, who had seen the distant land before it was cut away by the great water, and that when the water was low, many rocks were seen across it."

There are some striking points of resemblance between the Kampskadales and the Indians, but it is scarcely worth while to describe them here, alluding only to the habit of puncturing the flesh, and making figures upon it which they rub over with a blue liquid, and the marks become indelible. Bishop Lowth imagines this practice to be alluded to in Isaiah 49, 16. "Behold I have graven thee on the palms of my hand." The Jews at this time making representations of the City and Temple in their skins, to shew their affection for it, and retain its image in their minds.

Steller in his journal states that, "the main land of America lies parallel with the coast of Kampschatka, and they have the appearance of having been once joined, especially at the Cape. He assigns four reasons which induced him to think they were once united; the appearance of both coasts, which seem to have been torn asunder, many Capes which project into the sea, many small Islands which lie between them, the relative situation of those Islands, and the present breadth of the sea. From Bhering's Island, which lies in the middle,

M 3

both continents can be clearly seen even now: from all which it appears clearly, that there was once a passage, probably an easy one, from the one to the other land, either on the main before the separation took place, or from Island to Island at short distances or on the ice; and that the tribes of Israel wandering North-east and directed by the unseen hand of providence, or by some express tidings they, had received, thus entered into *a country wherein mankind never before dwelt.*

Dr. Robertson's remarks on these Straits, which had not the least reference to the subject of this volume, are however illustrative of the position here laid down. "The number of Volcanos in this part of the world is remarkable: there are several in Kampschatka, and not one of the Islands, great or small as far as the Russian navigation extends, is without them. Many are actually burning, and all the mountains bear marks of having been once in a state of irruption. Were I disposed to admit such conjectures as have found a place in other enquiries concerning the peopling of America, I might suppose, that this part of the earth, having manifestly suffered violent convulsions from earthquakes and volcanos, an isthmus, which formerly united Asia to America, has been broken and formed into an island by the shock." From the discoveries of Capt. Cook it appears, that within less than a degree of the polar circle these two continents present two opposite capes which are only thirteen leagues apart, in nearly the middle of which space lies Bhering's Island. Passing through this strait he saw distinctly the two continents lying on the right and left.

These tribes may not have gone thither alone. The alliances they had formed in Media might induce some other Easterns to accompany them; particularly their brethren who had been carried captive before them, and were in the same neighbourhood, and as much dissatisfied with the place of their banishment and with their oppressor's rod, as themselves. Others, natives of the Eastern coast, may have been driven by storms and cast upon the opposite Western land; and these considerations will furnish us with the means of accounting for a mixture of Asiatic language, manners and peculiarities.

How often do we read in ancient history, of very large bodies of people moving away from their ancient residence, either through choice or driven by a tyrant's command, to seek a new abode! When the warriors of the Northern nations invaded the South, they came accompanied by their wives and children, with the only habitations they could boast of, their tents, confident of obtaining better possessions in a more fertile and less encumbered country. The Israelites, with their flocks and families, were forty years finding their way into Canaan. When driven out by their Assyrian conquerors they were probably allowed but a small portion of their property to carry with them, but they went *en masse*, a distance of about 900 miles. Beyond them, in the vast regions of the North, was at that period but a very thin population, and we have reason to believe few or perhaps no settled habitations, towns or villages. The Scythians, whom Alexander could not conquer even on a more southern ground, must have been less and less thinly scattered as the country became more cold and less inviting. The Hebrew tribes were sent into their borders by the command of a Monarch, who at that time held a sovereign sway over an immense range of country as far North as what we now call Great Tartary, bordering upon a wild uncultivated track. The geographical situation of this country is worthy of attention. Media lay on the South-west side of the Caspian Sea stretching Northward beyond Armenia and Georgia; and, to the Northern-most quarter of this vast Empire, to Halah, Habor and Hara, on the river Gozan, these captives were sent. After the Assyrians, the Medes made themselves masters of that country, throwing off the Assyrian yoke. About one hundred years after which time the Scythians conquered the Median Empire in upper Asia, and retained the government about thirty years. Thus a time long enough elapsed to promote an acquaintance between the Northern parts of Media and the still more Northern country of Scythia or Tartary. It should be remarked, that the Russians did not get Siberia under their government until long after the period to which our attention is now directed.

While his power remained his captives would be compelled to keep their appointed station, but in after times when terror and confusion was spread through that country by the success of the Macedonian arms, and still more when the mighty conqueror had paid the debt of nature, leaving no heir to his crown, and his Generals became Kings and rivals among the Asiatic States, while they were waging war with one another and had more than enough to do to defend their own kingdoms from the aspiring chiefs; it does not appear that any obstacle would lie in the way of these Israelitish captives to move off in a direction contrary to that in which the civilized powers were keenly contesting for a mastery, through what might be called *no man's land*, to escape entirely from the hands of their enemies.

Possessed of the spirit of animosity which enflamed the breast of the Assyrian prince against these revolting tribes, after removing them to so great a distance from their own country, it is not probable that he would appoint them a place in the most fertile part of his dominions, but rather on its Northern frontier, yet thinly peopled, where their restless dispositions would place the peace of Media at no risk. And so it appears from history that he did.

Robertson, in his history of America, says of this country " that, if it was populated at all, it became so by the Sarmathians or Scythians. The land may be said to have belonged to none."

Some communication had always been kept up across the Northern parts of Asia in the way of trade, if it were only for the skins and the rich furs always in request in Babylon, and Assyria, and Persia. Through the means of merchants in these articles of commerce, some knowledge would be gained of countries lying at a distance, and the inhabitants of Media would not improbably learn that there was a country lying to the North-east which was visited for no other purpose than to obtain furs, in which were no human inhabitants. To the natives of Media and Persia this might be news of no interest, but in the proscribed race of Israel, robbed of a valuable and beloved

home, to which they could not look with the expectation
of a return, it might well awaken expiring hope : they
would listen with eagerness to all the reports which were
brought by travellers concerning it, they might even repeat the cautionary measure of the great leader of their
ancestors, and send some men in the character of traders
to spy out the land, and might eventually take advantage
of the confused state of Median and Macedonian politics
to slip away, with such means of subsistence as they could
procure: their immediate neighbours, happy to be released
from a large society of people whose manners were unlike
their own and whom they could regard in no other light
than conquered enemies. Than these none could be less
acceptable as neighbours. The inhabitants of Media and
Armenia might gladly act over again the part of the
Egyptians, and offer facilities to the escape of a people
whom they could not look upon with pleasure. Let us
pursue the object before us. In their progress there
would be little or nothing to impede them but the care
about provision, and one of the American traditions says
that they suffered great hardships : perhaps, as in their former pilgrimage so in this, all the souls died who went out of
Media, or perhaps some may have reached the land they
had promised themselves. But liberty was in their eye.
To be free from the state of anarchy in which they had
long been in Canaan through the attacks of their enemies,
and out of the hands of the tyrant who had robbed them
of their all, to enjoy independance in a wide range of land
where no one could oppress them, and in which provision of
various kinds was ready prepared to their hands—would be to

obtain a land flowing indeed with milk and honey—literally —and all their own, without even the danger of conquest. The idea of subjection to a foreign prince was always a galling load for a Hebrew to bear; the tributes they paid were the sorest of all their grievances. They are so to any nation, but were more especially so to these people who boasted of being immediately in God's keeping, and subject to no law but his, who held all idolaters in contempt and thought them the enemies of Jehovah. On their way to the Eastern shore they would meet now and then with travellers whose reports would revive their sinking spirits, and enable them to submit to privations and to suffer want, in the assurance that every day carried them nearer to the end of their march and that then their toils would be over. Vegetation of some sort would abound, wild animals might also range the forests and the wastes, and in whatever way the wandering Scythians lived, they might live in the same way. We who have been accustomed to a peaceful residence with civilized manners and plenty around, can form but a slight conception, scarcely any at all, of the manner in which the huge armies of Darius, of Alexander, of Xerxes, or of the Goths, were supported with their ten thousands of attendants. It has been often said that where an English Army would starve a French one would live well: if there be so much difference between those who in most points resemble each other, what may not be the difference between the means of maintaining at the present time a British population and those which were required for an Eastern mass of people two thousand years ago.

Among other traditions which have been met with is one upon the North-east coast of Asia, that very long ago, a large body of people coming out of the interior of the country did pass over into America, men, women and children.

And now let me direct the attention of my reader, not to the prophetical but the historical aid we receive from Scripture. The books of Esdras are not received into the Canon of Scripture; therefore I do not lay claim to divine authority, nor do I need it in reporting a plain fact known at the time of its being written, which was in the second century of the Christian æra; and evidently related by the writer with no design to impose a falsehood upon any one: for he could have no possible motive for venturing such a falsehood. In his second book 13. 50. we read. "And whereas thou sawest, that he, Jesus Christ, gathered another peaceable multitude unto him: those are the ten tribes, who were carried away prisoners out of their own land in the time of Osea, the King, whom Salmanazar, the King of Assyria, led away captive. And he carried them over the waters, and so they came into another land. But they took this council among themselves, that they would leave the multitude of the heathen, and go forth into a farther country where never mankind dwelt, that they might there keep their statutes, which they never kept in their own land. And they entered into Euphrates by the narrow passes of the river; for the Most High then shewed signs for them and held still the flood till they were passed over: for through that country there was a great way to go, namely, of a year and a half. And the same region is called Arsareth."

Euphrates was a term common with the Jews to signify a great river or body of water—this was in a country beyond that to which they were carried captive—God stopped the waters, froze them up, to let them pass—they went into a farther country where never man dwelt—and it was a great way off. All this account well corresponds with what has been said before, of the facilities which would offer themselves for their journey, and I think I may add, in the language of the mechanic, that it serves to dove-tail the statements already given, and to bring down my history in a clear and connected manner to that fatal war, which put an end to the Kingdom of Israel and gave a large and active population to the wilds, the woods, the mountains, and the Savannahs of a new world.

In reference to what has been stated at page 117, relative to the Copper-mine river, the place of landing in America, according to an ancient tradition, it may be observed, that near Bhering's Straits there is a place called Copper Island, from the vast quantities of that metal which are there found. In Grieve's history we are informed, that copper covers the shore in great abundance, so that ships might be loaded with the ore. In consequence of which report, the Gazetteer informs us, that an attempt was made in 1770 to obtain a load of it, but that the ice, even in July, was so abundant, and other difficulties so great, that the object was relinquished. There are other authorities to support this tradition, that in former times great quantities of copper were seen in those parts. And I will add, that the probability seems to be, that soon after the banishment of these tribes from their own land, into one of the very outskirts of the territory of their conqueror, they proceeded onward and reached this continent through the North-east passage: perhaps even before the captivity of the Jews. We have no reason given us to suppose, that they were carried captive for any use that the King of Assyria could make of them. They were not made slaves in his capital, nor employed in raising pyramids or other public works; but were placed where they would be out of the way of mischief. The captor appears to have wanted, not them, but their land, to complete his conquests: into which he sent a colony of his ancient subjects, to inhabit it, in whom he could place a greater confidence than he could place in a newly conquered nation, proud of supposed privileges and indignant of slavery.

CHAPTER IX.

ON THE ARTS AND THE SCIENCE OF THE INDIANS.

IT has been chiefly through the means of pious men of the United States, that we have been brought acquainted with the American Indians, and their acquaintance has been most intimately with those tribes which inhabited the back settlements, and the land lying towards the Pacific Ocean. These are the tribes which have discovered the least of civilization, they have dwelt in a country abounding in immense forests, which have been stored with a profusion of game and wild cattle of various kinds; and, being of a warlike character, have been at perpetual war with each other, and lived in a half savage, half civilized state, in the ordinary enjoyment of abundance; but, having no written means of instruction, have remained stationary, and have had no inclination to form themselves into better constructed and more enlightened society. But we are not therefore to conclude, that civilization has not taken place among any of these people; for on the contrary, it is well known, that there has been a great progress towards refinement, arts have been carried to a great extent, and there was a period, the date of which we cannot now ascertain, when Egypt herself could not furnish greater marks of industry, ingenuity and perseverance in the mechanic arts, than these people have exhibited.

These have been inquired into with great industry by Baron Humboldt, a native of Germany, whose Essays on the Kingdom of New Spain were published in New York in 1811. He ventures not any opinion on the origin of the people, but says that in New Spain, Peru, Canada, Florida and Brazil, there is a marked resemblance prevailing among them; and he adds, "In the faithful portrait which an excellent observer, Mr. Volney, has drawn of the Canada Indians, we recognize the tribes scattered in the meadows of Rio Apure and the Corona."

"They—the Mexicans before the Spanish conquest —had an almost exact knowledge of the duration of the year, and intercalated at the end of their great period of a hundred and four years with more accuracy than did the Greeks, Romans and Egyptians. The Taultees in the seventh and the Aztees in the twelfth centuries, as he learned from the hieroglyphical tables of the latter, which tables transmit to us the memory of the principal epochs of migration among the tribes, drew up the geographical map of the Country traversed by them; constructed cities, highways, dikes, canals, and immense pyramids very accurately designed, of 1416 feet in length. That of Cholula is 177 feet in height, it has four stories, lies exactly with the meridian, north and south, the width nearly equal to the length, and is composed of alternate strata of brick and clay. Many other pyramids are of the same construction but not so large, and bear a great resemblance to the temple of Belus at Babylon, and to the pyramids near Sackhara in Egypt. On that of Cholula is a Church surrounded by cypress : the length of the base is greater by almost half than that of the great pyramid Cheops, and exceeds all that are known on the old continent, and is constructed on a similar plan with them."

Humboldt adds. "How is it possible to doubt, that the Mexican nation had arrived at a certain degree of civilization, when we reflect on the care with which their hieroglyphical books were composed and kept; and recollect that a citizen of Thascala in the midst of the tumults of war took advantage of the facility offered him by the Roman alphabet, to write in his own language five large volumes on the history of a country, of which he deplored the subjection. Their hieroglyphical paintings, buildings of hewn stone, curious carvings in wood and works of sculpture still in preservation, though they do not discover any great excellence, yet bear a striking analogy to the monuments of more civilized people."

In the Archæologia Americana, containing Transactions and Collections of the American Antiquarian Society, published at Worcester in 1820, are described antiquities of the people who formerly inhabited the western parts of the United States : from these are taken the following extracts.

"The military works, the walls and ditches which cost so much labour in their structure, the numerous and tasty

mounds, which owe their origin to a people far more civilized than our Indians but far less so than Europeans, are
interesting on many accounts to the antiquarian, the philo-
sopher and the divine: especially when we consider
the immense extent of country which they cover, the great
labour which they cost their authors, the acquaintance with
the useful arts which they display, the grandeur of many
of the works themselves, and the traditionary accounts respecting them. They were once forts, cemeteries, temples,
altars, camps, towns, villages, race grounds, and other places
of amusement, habitations for chieftains, watch-towers
and monuments. From what we see of these works, the
people must have had some acquaintance with the arts and
sciences. They have left us perfect specimens of circles,
squares, octagons and parallel lines, on a great and noble
scale; and we also know, that they possessed the art of
working metals. Their wells, with stones at their mouths
remind us of those described in the patriarchal age."

"Near Newark, in Licking County, Ohio, between
two branches of the Licking river, at their junction, is one
of the most notable remains of the ancient works. It is
a fort inclosing forty acres, whose walls are ten feet high,
with eight gateways, each fifteen feet. Each gate guarded
by a wall placed before it. Near this fort was another
containing twenty two acres and connected with it by two
parallel walls of earth. Just without a gateway there is
an observatory so high as to command a view of the region
to a great distance; from which is a secret passage to an
ancient watercourse—other forts join to them, with watch-
towers surrounded by circular walls. These forts were

so placed as to enclose a number of large fields for culture, and appear to have had a communication with other forts by long parallel walls to the distance of many miles; the planning of which works of defence speaks volumes in favour of the sagacity of their authors. Tumuli, and some of them built of stone, are found about them. Pieces of earthenware, ornamented and glazed, pieces of copper and tools of iron are found in these works."

An account is given of several of this kind of military works, with various tools and instruments dug up from them, as spears, swords, knives, bricks well burned, mirrors of isinglass, stone axes and knives, ornaments of copper and of silver, a crucible that will still bear the usual heat, a stone pipe curiously wrought in high relief, on the front side a handsome female face. In the Tumuli have been found immense numbers of human bones, indicating a great population, or a vast destruction of life in war.

A writer in the Archæologia mentions one place, near the junction of the Ohio with the Missisippi, where are more than three thousand Tumuli, the largest of huge dimensions. "I have been sometimes induced," he says, "to think that at the period when these were constructed, there was a population as numerous as that which once animated the borders of the Nile or the Euphrates. I am perfectly satisfied that cities similar to those of ancient Mexico, of several hundred thousand souls, have existed in this country. Nearly opposite St. Louis, there are traces of two such cities in the distance of five miles."

Near Mexico are many pyramids which of themselves discover in the difficulty of their construction a vast population. There is a group of them in an adjoining valley, called the Path of the Dead, two large ones, surrounded by hundreds of smaller ones, which form square streets with the cardinal points of the compass. They are much in the style of the Egyptian pyramids. The two great ones had on their summit huge statutes of the sun and moon, formed of stone and covered with plates of gold, which the soldiers of Cortes plundered: these were not idols which they worshipped, as stated by the Spaniards, but emblems of the Great Spirit.

"About thirty years ago one of these pyramids was discovered by some hunters in a thick forest, built of hewn stone of a vast size and very beautiful; it has six or seven stories; three staircases lead to the top. The covering of its steps is decorated with hieroglyphical sculpture and small niches arranged with perfect symmetry."

In removing a large mound in Marietta bones of a person were found. "Lying immediately over, or on the forehead of the body, were found three large circular bosses, or ornaments for a sword belt, or a buckler; they are composed of copper, overlaid with a thick plate of silver. The fronts of them are slightly convex, with a depression, like a cup, in the centre, and measure two inches and a quarter across the face of each. On the back side, opposite the depressed portion, is a copper rivet or nail, around which are two separate plates, by which they were fastened to the leather. Two small pieces of the leather were found between the plates of one of the bosses." "Near the side of the body was found a plate of silver, which appears to have been the upper part of a sword scabbard; it is six inches in length and two in breadth, and weighs one ounce; it has no ornaments or figures, but has three longitudinal ridges, which probably correspond with the edges or ridges of the sword; it seems to have been fastened to the scabbard by three or four rivets, the holes of which yet remain in the silver.

"Near the feet was found a piece of copper weighing three ounces. From its shape it appears to have been used as a plumb, or for an ornament, as near one of the ends is a circular crease, or groove, for tying a thread; it is oblong, two inches and a half in length, one inch in diameter at the centre and half an inch at each end. It is composed of small pieces of native copper, pounded together; and in the cracks between the pieces are stuck several pieces of silver; one nearly the size of a four-penny piece, or half a dime. This copper ornament was covered with a coat of green rust, and is considerably corroded. A piece of red ochre, or paint, and a piece of iron ore, which has the appearance of having been partially vitrified, or melted, were also found. The ore is about the specific gravity of pure iron."

From the preceding facts it appears, that at some period previous to the arrival of the Spaniards in America, there had existed great and powerful nations in different parts of that continent, who were much advanced in the knowledge of Arts, possessed considerable mechanical genius, and understood Astronomy and Geography, to a much greater degree than any of the Inhabitants appeared to possess on their arrival; and had been highly civilized and polished nations, compared with all those of the Northern or Southern division of it: and that they had been destroyed by an irruption of the wild and wandering tribes; in a manner somewhat similar to what happened on the irruption of the Goths and Vandals in the Southern Kingdoms of Europe. With perhaps this difference that, like them, they neither received the polish of the conquered nor submitted to the laws of their religion. There always must be a general similarity of conduct in uncivilized people who are seeking conquest; but characteristic propensities may occasion some differences. And it has been remarked, that among the Indian tribes a strong and inconquerable hatred subsisted in time of war between some and others of them. So great was the disgrace attached to capture, that the warriors seldom suffered themselves to be taken prisoners. They either conquered or died: and many instances are known, of some of them which once were numerous being almost or entirely extirpated. Women and children were always spared and treated kindly by them; and, being adopted into their own tribes, were in future regarded as a part of them. And in this way we may well account for the destruction of the more enlightened nations; these ruins of whose towns, and forts, and pyramids &c., alone remain to give us a notion of what they were. The Indians of America have the character of being hostile to the neighbouring tribes: especially those that are the most rude. Having little to defend, they are the more jealous of any who might rob them of that little, and have ever discovered much of that fraternal animosity by which the children of Israel were distinguished; who fought, not only Judah

against Israel and Israel against Judah, with a deadly
hatred, but also one family of Israel against another family.
The tawny tribes of Africa are carrying on perpetual
skirmishings against each other; and it is, in order to
obtain prisoners to be converted into slaves of christian
men: but the Indians, like the Jews of old, wage wars of
extermination, and in this peculiar point, in which they
do not resemble any nation we are acquainted with, they
have the appearance of being of one kindred, and possessing one cruel and murderous mind. The King of Israel
could wage war against his brethren, and "slay in Judah
one hundred and twenty thousand in one day" who were all
valiant men, 2 Chro. 28. 5, "and carry captive two hundred
thousand women, sons and daughters, and bring them to
Samaria." And what could poor Indians do more?

The above remarks may apply with the greatest truth
to the Mexicans. It does not appear that the enlightened
inhabitants of Peru have been thus invaded by the hostile
tribes; for when Pizarro made the conquest of that country, they were in the enjoyment of a perfect peace, with
the monuments of their art and industry fresh around
them. The great labour of these vile invaders was, to
destroy all the marks of intellect which they found among
them, and reduce the people to a state of the most savage
ignorance. Accordingly we are told by Humboldt;

"That in order to reduce the intellectual character of
the natives as much as possible, and to make them so
much the more fit for the slavery to which they were devoted, all the better informed of the inhabitants, among
whom was a certain degree of intellectual culture, were

in one way or another destroyed by the invaders at the commencement of the conquest. Fanaticism—if that can be called by the name which in point of fact had, as we believe, little or no religion in it—was directed especially against the Priests, the Ministers of religion, and those who were connected with the houses of worship, who were the depositories of the historical, mythological and astronomical knowledge of the country. These people were completely annihilated, the more effectually to secure the cruel object of their ferocity; while the hieroglyphical paintings and other remains of learning, which transmitted from generation to generation the knowledge of their antiquities and of their religion, were carefully destroyed by the Monks. So that the people might be deprived of all their former means of religious instruction and of religious zeal, and an ignorance the most complete might overspread all that remained of the ancient race : which the christian Priests took effectual care to maintain."

"Long before the arrival of the Spaniards the natives of Mexico, as well as of Peru, were acquainted with the use of many of the metals. They did not content themselves with those which were found in their native state on the surface of the earth, in the beds of rivers or in the ravines formed by the torrents from the mountains : they had applied themselves to subterraneous operations in the working of veins, they had cut galleries and dug pits of communication and ventilation, and they had instruments adapted for cutting the rocks. Gold, silver, copper, lead and tin were publicly sold in some of their markets."

CHAPTER X.

ON the 18th of August, in the year 1644, a very small Book was published in Amsterdam, with the title, *The Gathering of Israel,* first written in Dutch by Manasseh Israel, and afterwards in Hebrew by Jacob, leader of the Synagogue of that City, for the benefit of the Jews generally. The Hebrew copy fell by mere accident lately into my hand; the contents of which I acquired by the assistance of a learned Jew of Plymouth. The writer was a man held in high esteem by the Hebrew people, and he gives a very good account of the person from whom he received the intelligence which occasioned his publishing the book, as a man worthy of credit, who did not appear to have any motive for giving a false account of his travels. This man's name was Aaron Levi, a Portuguese Jew. He was travelling on business, and came to the capital of Holland a short time before the publication made its appearance. His account is as follows. He had been at Honduras from whence he proceeded to Papuan, perhaps

Popayan, that is, he says, to Quito, where he hired mules of a Spaniard to go into the Country, and took with him a guide who was called Francisco. With him he proceeded towards the Cordilleras. Falling into conversation with his guide, he found him to be one of the original natives of America, who had much violence and injustice to charge the Spaniards with. He complained bitterly of their cruelties, and expressed not only a hope, but even a persuasion, that his countrymen would one day have the satisfaction of a revenge through the means of a people that were then concealed. Aaron's curiosity was much excited to know more of these people; and learning from his guide that some of them wore very long beards, others short ones, and that they observed the rite of circumcision, his anxiety greatly increased to see them, and he begged his guide to accompany him to the place where they resided. His guide consented, and he gave him three dollars to buy provisions, with a part of which money he purchased canvas shoes, and they began their journey. As they proceeded Francisco made many enquiries about Aaron's friends and origin. He asked him if he knew who was his original ancestor; to which Aaron replied yes, his name was Abraham, and added that he believed in one God that is in Heaven, and that all else that is said about God is false. Francisco then bound the stranger by an oath, that he would not betray him, either as to any thing he saw or any thing he heard, and that he would do as he directed him. Having travelled two days, the Indian made him put on the canvas shoes, take a staff and follow him.—He does not assign his reasons for this change; probably they were climbing the mountains, and the staff and the shoes were useful in their progress.—The Indian carried with him three measures of wheat and two ropes, in one of which were many knots and at the ends of them were short iron spikes, to throw (he says) among the rocks as they climbed up. On the Sabbath day they rested, and after two days journey more they arrived at the bank of a large river, much larger than the Douro. His guide then said to him, "here you will see your brethren." Having made a kind of flag with two pieces of cotton cloth, he waved it backward and forward, when a great smoke arose on the other side the river. "That smoke," said the Indian, "is a sign that they know we are here;" he then gave another sign, and three men and a woman came over in a little boat. Aaron did not understand the language in which these persons spoke, but his guide understood them: they looked hard in his face, expressed great pleasure at seeing him, and jumped about, and embraced, and kissed him. They said to him, and it was explained by Francisco, *The Lord is our God, the Lord is One.* see Deut. 6. 4. They used signs which the guide explained; they evidently knew that he was a Jew. They said Joseph dwells in the midst of the Sea, and held up two fingers, first joined together and then held apart, to intimate that they were two families descended from one head—Manasseh and Ephraim—and added, there will be a day on which we shall all meet: and you will tell our brethren, that you were the first that came here to us: no one of them has been here before you.

Upon this Aaron made a motion to get into the boat,

but they checked him, and, struggling with them, he fell into the water; they took him out, but refused to let him go over with them. For three successive days the boat continued to move to and fro across the water, bringing always four persons at a time; so that he supposed he saw about three hundred of them.

His account of the people is, that their countenances were much burned by the sun, that they were of a fine tall strait figure, many with beards, and that they wore on their heads a kind of turban. They gave directions to the Indian to tell him more about them, and then took their leave: on which the Jew and his guide returned to Quito.

On their way Aaron said to his guide, "now since you know a good deal about these people, you must tell me all you know, for they ordered you to tell me." The guide's answer was, "I will tell you the truth, and if you are not satisfied with what I tell you, and want to know more, I shall tell you false: what I know I learned from my ancestors, and it was handed down to them by tradition. The Almighty brought the children of Israel into this country by great miracles and wonderful works; if I told you all, you would think them contrary to nature. When we came into this country we had great battles with the people that lived here before us, and the wizards, of whom there were many among us, advised us to go to the place where those people whom you have just seen are, and make war against them; which we did, and all our army was destroyed. Then we gathered a larger army and fought with them; and that army was also cut off. A third time we collected all our men of war together, and none of them returned alive. We then thought that the wizards had given this advice through spite; and they that remained rose against them and killed a great many of them: the others begged for their life, which was granted, on condition of their telling them the truth. Then the old men taught us, that the God of the children of Israel is the true God, and that his commandments are true; and that a time will come when these people will have rule over the whole earth. Peace was then made between us all, on condition that we should never pass over the river to them, but that every seventeen moons one of their people should come amongst us, to make us a visit and enquire about our prosperity, and that the secret of their concealment should not be revealed to any one who was not three hundred moons old; that it should never be revealed in any house, but in the field in the open air, that none might overhear. There has been communication between them and us only three times; the first when the Spaniards came over into the country, the second when ships came into the sea of Zur, and the third time is the present of your coming."

The above historical circumstances are related in the preface to the little book, which forms a comparatively large portion of it: after which the Author proceeds to make remarks on the Narrative of Aaron Levi. He says that before this time it was quite out of his power to obtain any satisfactory information of the ten tribes. He had read several accounts of them, but could rely upon none. He quotes some of these accounts, giving the particulars, and his reasons for discrediting them. One of them, Arias Montana, says, "The language of the Peruvians is the same as our language."

The Jews receive and acknowledge four books of Ezra, written in the time of Hosea; the first is that which is in our Bible; in the fourth Ezra writes—"that the ten tribes were solicitous to find a place in which they might remain quiet and at peace. So they passed over the Euphrates, God performing a miracle and stopping the water, that they might pass safely over. They then came to a country called Arsaret, which is Great Tartary, and passing through it they arrived at an Island called Grona, from whence they crossed a narrow passage to a land called Labrador, which is India." The passage already quoted from Esdras has much the appearance of having been taken from it.

Another writer says, "Arsaret is the outer part of the continent, which is Tartary on the Sea, and that Plyneas writes, that from thence there is a narrow passage over to another land."

Another writer mentions the fact, "that the Spaniards found a tombstone in Mexico which was engraven in the Hebrew language, that the customs of the American Indians where just like those of the Jews, and that some of them were known to use the *rite of circumcision*." Upon the whole this writer appears fully satisfied, that by some means or other a considerable portion of the ten tribes went over into America; and thinks it probable, that Reuben, Gad and Manasseh, which were taken away in the first captivity, and placed among the Mountains of

Media, by the King of Ashur, were the earliest to go there. And that they were afterwards followed by the men of the second captivity.

Here is an evidence, coming in an oblique direction, which carries with it, as I conceive, great conviction, that it was known to the learned among the Jewish people two hundred years ago, scarcely half a century after the conquest of Peru, that some of their brethren, of whom they had long lost sight, were safely settled in the continent of America: that the fate of these people had engaged the attention of many of their writers, who had solicitously enquired after their destination; and that at last, one who held a high rank among them, published in his own language a little book, for the express purpose of declaring, that, although he had hitherto been ignorant of their fate, he was then satisfied, by evidence which he saw no reason to discredit, that at least a part of them were safely established as a separate people among the vast range of the Cordilleras.

There is considerable difficulty in deciphering some of the proper names which are found in this little book: the Hebrew characters not corresponding exactly with the English, and the manner of writing the words depending on the reporter's pronunciation, and the names of places and of countries not being the same two hundred years ago, in the languages in which the books were written, that they are now in our Atlas.

Another remark may be of some interest to the reader: whether when these people made use of the passage that is found in Deuteronomy, *The Lord is our God, the Lord is*

One, they would, had they been permitted, have used the word Jehovah. But the reporter could not inform us of this very important fact, which would so clearly illustrate the subject; for no Jew is allowed to write that word on any occasion whatever, except in copying the books of Moses, nor to utter it on any such an occasion: and, when the word occurs in reading any part of those books in the Synagogue on the Sabbath day, they always substitute for it the term *adonai*. Admitting even that they were of the Hebrew nation, they must have said, and Jacob must have written, adonai.

The Indian, who acted as interpreter on this occasion, spoke of people who were in the country when his ancestors arrived in it; which may lead some to suppose, that these Hebrew tribes were not the first to colonize the American continent, or at least that part of it which lies below the Cordilleras towards the sea. It is not clear however from this man's relation, that they carried on war against any but those on the other side the river, nor is any motive assigned for their attempting to disturb them in their settlement. If the supposition of this learned Jew be correct, it will appear, that the first persons who came there were the descendants of Manasseh and Ephraim who stationed themselves beyond the river, and that some other wanderers of the same migration afterwards settled in Peru, and having skirmished awhile with their neighbours, ultimately formed the kingdom which sprang up and was consolidated under the Incas; a peaceful and happy nation.

The term Wizard used by the Indian is, in this little

book, the same word as is found in the Hebrew Bible and translated Wizard in ours: an order of men for whom the degenerate Israelites had a high regard, and to whom they applied habitually for advice in all difficult cases; as appears from many denunciations of the Prophets. And, as Moses in his law guarded them against their impositions, and forbade the people to apply to them, it would appear; that they brought with them some of this order into the land of promise, who had learned their magic arts in Egypt; that they retained them in the land of Canaan, where they recovered their plenary power under the Idolatrous Kings of Israel; and that they still preserved that power after they had emigrated to the new world. Their ancient priests had been long neglected; but wizards and necromancers were still in esteem. That the people finding themselves deceived by the wizards, who we are to suppose were numerous and forming an order in the state, should rise against them and kill a great many of them, is exactly what their ancestors had been every now and then in the habit of doing with their ghostly advisers. One time it was the Priests of the Lord who were slain by scores and by hundreds: another it was the Priests of Baal who fell in crowds: and again we read, of all the witches and wizards of the land being put to death. Such was the spirit of this people: they were always a murderous set.

When we find that the Jewish nation had entirely lost sight of their brethren, the Children of Israel, and had not been able before the period in which this little book was written to obtain any information as to what had become of them, we need not wonder that Christian writers were at an utter loss to account for their entire disappearance; that Prideaux should unhesitatingly declare, that they were merged and lost in the Asiatic tribes; and that Gibbon should give himself no trouble to account for the total destruction of a nation once so peculiar in their habits, so deeply rooted in national prejudice, and so distinguished as these descendants of the Hebrew people were. His proud and unbelieving spirit would perhaps grudge the labour of research after them. The ruler of the Synagogue at Amsterdam had been interested in the question of their final destiny; he could not be satisfied that they had been abandoned by their Almighty Friend, and had taken pains to search into every thing that had been written concerning them : but without success.

It is only by uniting facts which time brings to light, that circumstances of so mysterious a nature, as the disappearance of this great body of people, can find an explanation; and then it is the bearing of one discovery upon another, and their leading to the developement, rather than a direct and clear evidence, that unfolds the hidden secret and brings satisfaction to the mind.

CHAPTER XI.

THE INVASION OF CORTES.

IN the year 1578, a book was published in London with the title, "The Pleasant Historie of the Conquest of the VVeast India, now called new Spayne, Atchieued by the vvorthy Prince Hernando Cortes, Marques of the valley of Huaxacat, most delectable to Reade."

This is a translation from the Spanish, and is printed in the old English Black Letter. I have it in my possession and esteem it a curiosity. It betrays too surely both the indisposition of the Spaniards to think, or at least, to speak justly of those truly interesting people, the pains they took to misrepresent them, either through ignorance or base design, and the steady and persevering use Cortes made of the name of Religion, as a plea for his usurpation and apology for all his cruelties. Throughout this book they are represented as idolaters of the basest kind; they are charged with sacrificing thousands of their enemies and also of their own people to their deity; they are spoken of as constantly and ordinarily feeding on human carcases; and, to crown all, it is the Devil who is their favorite deity and chief adviser, in all the steps they were induced to take to resist these worthy christians; who came to visit them with no other design than to make them cease from human sacrifice, give up the worship of the Devil, and receive the glad tidings of Salvation through Christ Jesus. It is a heart-rending history indeed that even this Spaniard writes, whose object it was to show his companions' behaviour in the fairest colours. No one can read it, who has obtained information respecting that degenerate race of men from other quarters, without perceiving an entire plan of deception carried on, from the time that Cortes first landed at Ulhua to the complete conquest of the rich town of Mexico. A few extracts from this work may amuse the reader.

The Oration that Cortes made to his Soldiers.—"My louing fellowes and déere friendes, it is certayne that euery valiant manne of stoute courage, doth procure by déedes to make him selfe equall with the excellente men of his time, yea and with those that were before his time. So it is, that I do now take in hand such an enterprise, as god-willing shall be héereafter of greate fame, for myne heart doth pronosticate vnto mée, that we shall winne greate and rich Countreys, and manye people, as yet neuer séene to anye of oure nation, yea and (I béeliue) greater kingdomes than those of oure kinges. And I assure you, that the desire of glory dothe further extend, than treasure, the whiche in sorte, mortall life doth obtayne. I haue now prepared Shippes, Armor, Horses, and other furniture for the warres, with victuall sufficient, and all things that are

vsed as necessary in Conquestes. I haue bin at greate
costes and charges, wherein I haue not onely employed
myne owne goodes, but also the goodes of my friendes, yet
me thinketh that the employmente thereof dothe encrease
my treasure and honor. We ought (louing fellowes) to
leaue off small things, when great matters doe offer themselues. And euen as my trust is in God, euen so greater
profite shall come to our kings, and a nation of this oure
enterprise, than hath héertofore of any other. I doe not
speake how acceptable it will be to God our sauiour, for
whose loue I do chiefly and willingly hazard my goods and
trauel. I will not nowe treat of the perils and danger of
life that I haue passed since I began this voyage. This
I say, that good men doe rather expect renoune, than treasure. We doe now attempt and begin warre that is both
good and iust, and the almighty God in whose name and
holy faith this voyage is begonne, will assuredly graunte
vnto vs victory, and the time will shew the end of things
well begonne."

On an island called Acusamil they met with a Spaniard,
who gave the following account of himself—" Sir, my
name is *Geronimo de Aguilar,* I was borne in the Cittie
of *Esya* in the *Andolozia,* and by misfortune I was
loste after this sorte. In the warres of *Darien* and in the
time of the contentions and passions of *Iames de Nicuessa*
and *Vasco Nonez Balboa,* I came with Captaine *Valdinia*
in a little Caruell, toward *Santo Domingo,* to giue aduice
to the Admirall and gouernour, of the troubles which had
happened, and my comming was for men and victuals :
and likewise we brought twentye thousand Duckettes of

the kings in *Anno* 1511. And when we apported at *Ia-mayca,* our Caruel was lost on the shallowes whiche were called the Uipars, and with greate pain we entred (about twenty persons) into the boate, with out sayle, water or bread, and weake prouission of oares : we thus wander thirtéene or fourtéene dayes, and then the currant, whiche is there very great & runneth alway weastward, cast vs a shoare in a prouince called *Maya,* & trauelling on our way, seauen of our fellowes died wyth hunger & famin. And captain *Valdinia* & other 4. were sacrifised to the ydols by a cruel and cursed *Cacike,* that is to say, a Lord in whose power we fell, &c.

"And after the sacrifice, they were eaten among the *In-dians* for a solemne banket : and I, and other sixe wer put into a Cage or coupe, to be fatned for an other sacrifice. And for to escape suche abhominable death, we brake the prison and fledde through certaine mountaines : So that it pleased God that wee mette with another *Cazike* who was enimy to him that first toke vs, his name was *Quin-qus,* a man of more reason and better condition, hee was Lord of *Xamansana :* he accepted vs for his captiues, but shortly after he dyed, and then I aboad with *Taxmar* his heire. Then deceased other fiue of our fellowes, so that there remayned but only I and one *Gonsalo Guerrer,* a maryner, who now abydeth with *Nachancan* the Lorde of *Chetemal,* and he married with a rich gentlewoman of that countrey, by whom he hath children, and is made a Captaine, and wel estéemed with the *Cazike* for the victo-ries that he hath had in the wars against the other Lords. I sent vnto him your worships letter, desiring him that he

would come with me hauing so fit a passage, but he refused my request, I belieue for verye shame, because hee
had his nose ful boared of holes, & his eares iagged, hys
face & handes painted according to the vse of the countrey,
or else he abode there for the loue he bare to his wife and
children." 'All those whiche stoode by & hard this Historie,
were amased, to heare *Geronimo de Aguilar* report howe
those *Indians* did sacrifise & eate mans flesh. They also la-
mented the miserie & death of his fellowes, and highly
praysed God, to see him free from his bondage & from such
cruel & barbarous people, & to haue likewise so good an
enterpreter with them, for vndoubtedly it semed a miracle
the *Aluarados* ship fel into a leak, for with the extremity
they returned back again to that Iland, wheras with contra-
rie winde they were constrayned to abide the coming of
Aguilar, and certainly he was the mean & spéech of al their
procéedings. And therfore haue I bin so prolixious in the
rehearsal of this matter. as a notable point of this historie.
Also I wil not let to tell how the mother of *Geronimo de
Aguilar*, became mad. &c.'

'When she hard that hir son was captiue among people
who vsed to eate mans flesh, & euer after when she saw
any flesh spitted or roasted, she would make an open out-
crie, saying, oh I miserable woman, behold this is the flesh
of my dearebeloued sonne who was all my comfort.'

The account given of this island is that 'It contayneth
ten leagues in length & thrée leagues in breadth, although
some say more, some lesse : it standeth twentye degrees on
this side the equator, and fiue leagues from the womens
cape : it hath thrée villages, in the which liueth nere 3 thou-

sand men. The houses are of stone and brick, and couered with straw & bowes, & some with tile. Their temples and towers are made of lime & stone very wel built : thei haue no other fresh water but out of welles and raine water. *Calachuni* is their chiefe Lord : they are browne people & goe naked : & if any weare cloth, it is made of cotten wool only to couer their private members : they vse long hear platted & bound about their foreheads : they are great fishermen, so the fish is their chiefest foode & sustenance, they haue also *Maiz* which is for bread : also good fruites : & hony, but somewhat soure : and plots for bées, which contayn. 1000 hiues. They knew not to what use wax serued, but when they saw our men make candels thereof, they wondred thereat. Their dogges haue Foxe faces and barke not, these they gelde and fatten to eate. This Iland is ful of high mountaines, & at the feete of them, good pastures many Deare and wilde Boares, Connyes and Hares, but they are not great. The Spaniardes with their handguns and crossebowes prouide them of that victual, fresh salt and dried. The people of this *Iland* are Idolaters, they doe sacrifice children, but not manye. And many times in stead of children they sacrifice dogges. They are poore people, but very charitable and louing in their false religion and beliefe.'

'The religion of the people of *Acusamil.*—The temple is like vnto a square Toure broad at the foote, & steps round about it, & from the middest upward very straight : the top is hollow and couered with straw : it hath foure windowes with frontals and galleries. In the holow place is their chappel, wheras their Idols do stand.

The temple that stoode by the sea side was such a one, in the which was a maruellous straunge Idol, and differed muche from all the rest, although they haue manye and of diuerse fashions. The body of this Idol was great and hollow, and was fastened in that wall with lime: hee was of earth. And behinde this Idols backe was the Uesterie, where was kept ornaments & other things of seruice for the temple. The priests had a little secret dore hard adjoining to the Idol, by which dore they crept into the hollow Idol, and answered the people who came with prayers & peticions. And with this deceit the simple soules beleued al the Idol spake, and honored the god more then al the rest with many perfumes and swéete smelles, and offered bread and fruite, with sacrifice of Quayles bloud, and other birds, and dogges, and sometime mans bloud. And through the fame of this Idoll and Oracle, many Pilgrimes came to *Acusamil* from many places. At the foote of this Temple was a plotte like a Churchyard, well walled and garnished with proper pinnacles, in the middest whereof stoode a Crosse of ten foote long, the which they adored for God of the rayne, for at all times when they wanted rayne, they would goe thither on Procession deuoutely, and offered to the Crosse Quayles sacrificed, for to appease the wrath that the God séemed to haue agaynste them: and none was so acceptable a sacrifice, as the bloud of that little birde. They vsed to burne certaine swéete gume, to perfume that God withall, and to besprinkle it with water, and this done, they beléeued assuredly to haue rayne. Suche is the Religion of those *Indians* of *Acusamil*. They could neure know the original how that God of Crosse came amongst them, for in all those parties of *India*, there is no memorie of anye Preaching of the Gospell that had bin at any time, as shall be shewed in another place.'

Similar descriptions are given of other towns. Next follows a description of a temple found on the Continent.

'There was in that Village a temple, whiche hadde a little Tower with a Chappell on the toppe, and twentie steppes to come unto the Chappell, where they found some Idolles, and many bloudy papers, and much mans bloud of those which hadde bin sacrificed, as Marina did certifie. They found also the blocke whereupon they used to cutte open the menne sacrificed, and the razors made of Flint; wherewyth they opened their breasts and plucked out their heartes beeyng aliue throwing them uppe toward Heaven as an offering, and after this done they anoynted their idolles and the papers they offered, and then burned them.'

'From the passage of the river they had a faire way to another river, which being likewise waded ouer, they discried Zempoallan, whiche stoode a myle distant from them, all beset with fayre Orchardes and Gardens, verye pleasaunte to beholde, they used always to water them with sluses when they pleased. There proceeded out of the towne many persons, to behold an receyue so strange a people unto them. They came with smiling countenance and presented unto them diuers kinde of floures and sundry fruites, which none of our men had heeretofore seene. These people came without feare among the ordinance; with this pompe, triumph, and ioy they were receiued into the Citie, which seemed a beautifull Garden, for the trees were so greene and high that scarsely the houses appeared.'

From Vera Crux, the first town the Spaniards built, rich presents were sent to the Court of Spain, many articles in gold, silver, feathers and wood, curiously wrought, with carpets and cloth of cotton.

'All these things wer more beautiful than rich : the workmanship of al was more worth than the thing it selfe. The colours of the cloth of cotton wool was exceeding fine and the fethers natural.'

'The pounced worke in gold and siluer exceed ovr goldsmithes. They joyned to this present certaine Indian bookes of figures which serve to their use for letters ; these bookes are folden like unto clothes, and written on both sides. Some of these books were made of cotton and glewe, and others were made of leaves of a certain tree called Melt, whyche serue for theyr paper, a thing straunge to behold.'

The Country of Tlaxcallan was separated from that of Mexico ' by a greate circuite of stone made without lyme or mortar, being a fathom and a half high and twentie foote brode, with loupe holes, to shoot at : that wall crossed ouer all the valley from one mountayne to another, and but one only entrance or gate, in the which the one wall doubled against the other, and the way there was fourtie paces brode, in such sort, that it was an euil and perilous passage, if any had bene there to defend it.'

'They have all kinde of good policie in the citie ; there are Goldsmithes, Fetherdressers, Barbors, Hotehouses, and Potters, who make as good earthen vessel as is made in Spayne.'

Chololla, a place they passed through in their way to
Mexico 'is called the Sanctuary or holy place among the
Indians, and thither they trauelled from many places
farre distante on pilgrimage, and for this cause were many
temples. It sheweth outwards verye beautifull and full
of towers, for there are as manye temples as dayes in the
yeare, and every temple hath his towers. Our men counted foure hundred towers. The men and women are of good
dispositions, well fauoured and very wittie.' We learn
that when Mutezuma heard of the taking of Chololla,
he feared and said, "These are the people that our
Gods said should come and inherite this land." 'He
went incontinent to his oratore and shut himself alone,
where he abode in fasting and prayer eyght dayes, with sacrifice of many menne to asslake the fury of his idolles,
who seemed to be offended. The voyce of the Diuell
spake unto him, bidding him not to feare the Christians &c.'

I shall here subjoin the speech of Mutezuma to Cortes
and his company.

"Lorde and Gentlemen.—I doe much rejoyce to haue
in my house such valiant men as ye are, for to vse with
curtesie, and entreate you with honour, according to your
desert and my estate. And where heretofore I desire'd
that you shoulde not come hither, the onely cause was my
people had a greate feare to sée you, for your gesture and
grimme beards did terrifie them, yea, they reported that
yée had such beastes as swallowed men, and that your
coming was from heaven, bringing with you lightning,
thunder and thunderbolts, wherwith you made the earth
to tremble and to shake, and that yée slew therewith whom

ye pleased. But now I do sée and know that ye are mortall men, and that ye are quiet and hurt no man: also I haue séene your horses, which are but your seruauntes, and youre Gunnes lyke vnto shootyng Trunkes. I do now hold all for fables and lyes which hath bin reported of you, and I do also accept you for my méere kinsmen. My father tolde me that hée had heard his forefathers say, of whome I doe descende, that they helde opinion howe they were not naturals of thys lande, but come hither by chance, in companye of a mighty Lorde, who after awhile that they hadde abode héere they returned to their natiue soyle: After manye yeares expired, they came agayne for those whome they had left héere behind them, but they would not goe wyth them, because they had héere inhabited, and hadde wyues and children, and great gouernement in the land. Nowe these myghtie Lordes séeyng that they were so stubborne, and woulde not returne with them, departed from them sore displeased, saying, that he woulde sende his children that should both rule and gouerne them, in iustice, peace, and auntient Religion, and for this consideration, wée haue always expected and beléeued, that suche a people should come to rule and gouerne us, and considering from whence you come, I doe think that you are they whome we looked for, and the notice which the greate Emperour *Charles* had of vs, who hath now sent you hither. Therefore Lorde and Captayne, be well assured, that we wyll obey you, if there be no fayned or deceytfull matter in your dealings, and will also deuide wyth you and youres all that we haue. And although this which I haue sayde were not only for youre vertue, fame, and déedes of valiant Gentlemen, I would yet do it for your worthinesse in the battayles of *Tauasco, Teocaz-inco,* and *Chollola,* béeying so few, to ouercome so many."

"Now agayne, if ye ymagine that I am a God, and the walles and roufes of my houses, and all my vessell of ser-uice to be of pure golde, as the men of *Zempoallan, Tlax-callan,* and *Huexozinco* hath enformed you, it is not so, and I iudge you to be so wise, that you giue no credit to such fables. You shall also note, that through your commyng hither, manye of my subiects haue rebelled, and are be-come my mortall enimies, but yet I purpose to breake their wings. Come féele you my body, I am of fleshe and bone, a mortal man as others are and no God, although as a king I doe estéeme my selfe of a greater dignitie and preheminence than others. My houses you do also see which are of tymber and earthe, and the principallest of Masons worke, therefore nowe you do both knowe and sée what odious lyars those talebearers were. But troth it is, that golde plate, feathers, armour, iewels, and other riches, I haue in the treasory of my forefathers a long time preserued, as the vse of kings is, all the which you & yours shal enioy at all times. And now it may please you to take your rest, for I know that you are wéery of your iourney." *Cortez* with ioyfull countenance humbled him-selfe, séeyng some teares fall from *Mutezuma* his eyes, saying vnto him, "Vppon the trust I haue hadde in youre clemencye, I insisted to come both to sée and talke wyth your highnesse, and now I know that all are lyes which hath bin tolde me. The like youre highnesse hath hearde reported of vs, assure youre selfe, that the Emperoure Kyng of *Spayne* is your naturall Lorde, whome yée haue expected for, he is the onely heyre from whence youre ly-nage dothe procéede, and as touching the offer of youre highnesse treasure, I do most hartyly thanke you."

'The Maiestie and order, vvherevvith Mutezuma was serued:—Mutezuma was a man of small stature and leane, his couloure tawnie as all the *Indians*, are. He hadde long heare on hys heade, six little heares vppon him, as though they hadde bin put in with a bodkin. His thinne bearde was blacke. Hée was a man of a fayre condition, and a doer of Justice, well spoken, graue and wise, beloued and feared among his subjectes. *Mute Zuma* doth signifie sadensse.'

'To the proper names of Kings and Lords, they do adde this sillable C. which is for cortesie and dignitie, as we vse Lord. The Turke vseth *Zultan.* The Moore or Barbarian calleth his Lorde *Mulley,* and so the *Indians* say *Mute Zuma Zin.* His people hadde him in such reuerence, that he permitted none to sit in his sight, nor yet in his presence to weare shoes, nor looke him in the face, except very few Princes. He was glad of the con-uersation of the *Spanyardes* and would not suffer them to stande on foote, for the great estimation he had of them, and if he lyked any of the *Spanyardes* garments, he woulde exchange his apparrell for theirs.'

'He changed his owne apparrell four times euery day, and he neuer clothed himselfe agayne with the garments which he hadde once worne, but all suche were kepte in his Guardrobe, for to giue in presents to his seruantes

and Ambassadors, and vnto valiante souldyers which
had taken any enimie prisoner, and that was esteemed
a great reward, and a title of priuiledge.

'Then follow an account of suitors who applied to the
King, who having their answers returned backward not
turning their tayles to the Prince, after which followed
players, who play with their feete as we doe with oure
handes: also other plays, throwing cudgels into the air:
they have a kind of bean squared like dice and marked, at
which game they play all that they haue and many tymes
they valew theyr owne bodyes and play that into captivi-
tie. To which succeeds an account of a tennis court, in
which the King amused himself with a ball made of gum,
hard, black, but excellent to rebound. He is represented
as having a thousand women, gentlewomen, servants and
slaves, the most noblemen's daughters. Mutezuma took
for himself those he liked best and gave the rest in marriage to Gentlemen, his servants. His palace was of an
immense extent with courts, a hundred bathes and hot-
houses, worked with great art and beauty, a house of foule
for hawking, others kept only for their feathers, together
with animals of all kinds in abundance, snakes and lizards
and adders and lions—though there certainly were no lions
in America—and wolves and tigers, howling and barking
to the great terror of the Spaniards, who saw the floure
couered with bloud like a slaughter house, it stonke
horribly.

'Moste certaine, in the nighte season it séemed a Don-
geon of Hell, and a dwelling place of the Deuill, and even
so it was indéede, for neare at hande was a Hall of a

hundred and fiftie foote long, and thirtie foote broad, where was a Chappell with the Roofe of siluer and gold in leafe Wainescotted, and decked with greate store of pearle and stone, as Agattes, Cornerines, Emeraldes, Rubies, and diuerse other sortes, and thys was the Oratory where *Mutezuma* prayed in the nighte season, and in that chappell the Diuell did appeare vnto hym, and gaue him answere according to his prayers.'

The description of his armory, his gardens, his court and body guard exhibit him as a most powerful and splendid monarch, to whom the noblemen paye their tribute in personal service, the husbandmen with body and goodes.

'The great Temple of Mexico.—The Temple is called *Teucalli*, that is to say, Gods house, *Teurl* signifieth God, and *Calli* is a house, a vowell very fitte, if that house had bene of the true God. The Spaniards that vnderstand not the language, do pronounce and call those Temples *Cues*, and the God *Vitzilopuchtli, Vchilobos*. There are in *Mexico* many parishe churches, with towers, wherein are Chappells and Altares where the images and idols do stande, and those chappells do serue for burial places of their founders, and the Parishioners are buried in the Church-yarde. All their Temples are of one fashion, therefore it shal be nowe sufficient to speake of the cathedral church. And euen as those temples are al in generall of one making in that citie. I doe beleue that the lyke was neur séene nor harde off. This temple is square, and doth containe euery way as much ground as a crossebow can reach leuell: it is made of stone, with foure dores that abutteth

Q

vpon the thrée calseys, and vpon an other parte of the Cittie, that hath no calsey but a fayre streate.'

'In the middest of this Quadern standeth a mount of earth and stone square lykewise, and fiftie fadom long euery way, buylte vpwards like vnto a pyramide of Egipt, sauyng the toppe is not sharpe, but playne and flatte, and tenne fadom square: vpon the weast side, were steppes vp to the toppe, in number an hundreth and fourtene, whiche beying so many, high, and made of good stone did séeme a beautifull thing. It was a straunge sight to beholde the Priests, some going vp, and some downe with ceremonies, or with men to be sacrificed. Upon the toppe of this Temple are two great Alters, a good space distant the one from the other, and so nigh the edge or brimme of the wall, that scarcely a man mought go behind them at pleasure. The one Alter standeth on the right hande, and the other on the left, they were but of fiue foote highe, eche of them had the backe part made of stone, paynted with monstrous and foule figures, the Chappell was fayre and well wrought of Masons worke and timber, euery Chappell had thrée loftes one aboue another, susteyned vpon pillers, and with the height thereof it shewed like vnto a fayre tower, and beautified the Cittie a farre of: from thence a man mought sée all the cittie and townes rounde aboute the lake, whiche was undoubtedly a goodly prospect. And because *Cortes* and his company should sée the beautie thereof, *Mutezuma* brought him thither, and shewed hym all the order of the Temple, euen from the foote to the toppe. There was a certaine plot or space for the idol Priests to celebrate their seruice without disturbance of any. Their general prayers were made toward the rising of the sunne. Upon ech alter standeth a great idoll. Beside this tower that standeth vpon the pyramide, there are fourtie towers great and small belonging to other little temples which stand in the same circuite, the which although they were of the same making, yet theyr prospect was not westwarde, but otherwayes, bicause there should be a difference betwixte the great temple and them. Some of these Temples were bigger than others, and euery one of a seuerall God, among the whiche there was one rounde temple dedicated to the God of the ayre called *Quecalcouatl,* for euen as the ayre goeth rounde aboute the heauens, euen for that consideration they made his temple rounde. The entrance of that Temple had a dore made lyke vnto the mouth of a Serpent, and was paynted with foule and Dieulish gestures, with great téeth and gummes wrought, whiche was a thing to feare those that should enter in thereat, and especially the Christians vnto whom it represented very Hel with that ougly face and monsterous téeth.'

'There were other *Teucalles* in the citie that had the ascending vp by steps in thrée places : all these temples had houses by themselues with all seruice and priests and particular Gods. At euery dore of the great temple standeth a large Hall and goodly lodgings, both high and lowe round about, which houses were common armories for the Citie, for the force and strength of euery towne is the temple, and therefore they haue there placed their storehouse of munition. They had other darke houses full of idols, greate and small, wrought of sundry mettals, they

aie all bathed and washed with bloud, and do shewe very
black through theyr dayly sprinklyng and anointing them
with the same, when any man is sacrificed: yea and the
walles are an inch thicke with bloud, and the grounde is a
foote thicke of bloud, so that there is a diuelish stench.
The Priests or Ministers goe daylye into those Oratories,
and suffer none others but great personages to enter in.
Yea and when any such goeth in, they are bounde to
offer some man to be sacrificed, that those bloudy hangmen
and ministers of the Diuell may washe their handes in
bloud of those so sacrificed, and to sprinkle their house
therewith.'

' For their seruice in the kitchen they haue a ponde of
water that is filled once a yéere, which is brought by conduct from the principal fountayne. All the residue of the
foresayde circuite serueth for places to bréede foule, with
gardens of hearbes and swéete trées, with Rose and
floures for the Alters. Such, so great and straunge was
this temple of *Mexico,* for the seruice of the Diuell who
had decieued those simple *Indians.* There dothe reside
in the same temple continually fiue thousand persons, and
all they are lodged and haue theyr living there, for that
temple is maruelous riche, and hath diuers townes onely
for their maintainaunce and reparation, and are bounde to
sustayne the same alwayes on foote. They doe sowe
corne, and maintayne all those fiue thousande persons
with bread, fruyte, flesh, fish and firewoodde as much as
they néede, for they spende more fire-woodde than is spent
in the kings courte: these persons doe liue at their hartes
ease, as seruauntes and vassals vnto the Goddes. *Mute-*

zuma brought *Cortes* to this temple, because his men shoulde sée the same, and to enforme them of his religion and holinesse, wherof I will speake in an other place, being the most straunge and cruellest that euer was harde off.'

The Idols of Mexico.—'The Gods of *Mexico,* were two thousand in number, as the *Indians* reported, the chieftest were *Vitcilopuchtli* and *Tezcatlispuca,* whose images stoode highest in the Temple vppon the Altars: they were made of stone in ful proportion as bigge as a Gyant. They were couered with a lawne called *Nacar.* These images were besette with pearles, precious stones, and péeces of gold, wrought like birds, beastes, fishes, and floures adorned with Emeralds, Turquies, Calcedons, and other little fine stones, so that when the lawne *Nacar* was taken away, the Images séemed very beautiful to beholde.'

'The Image had for a girdle great snakes of gold, and for collors or chaynes about their necks, ten hartes of men, made of golde. and each of those Idolles had a counterfaite visor with eyes of glass, and in their necks death painted: eache of these things hadde their considerations and meanings. These two Goddes were brethren, for *Tezcatlispuca* was the God of Providence, and *Vitcilopuchtli* God of the warres, who was worshipped and feared more than all the rest.'

'There was another God, who hadde a greate Image placed vppon the toppe of the Chappell of Idols, and hée was esteemed for a speciall and singular God aboue all the reste. This God was made of all kinde of séedes that groweth in that Countrey, and being ground, they made a certayne past, tempered with childrens bloud, and Virgins sacrificed, who were opened with their razures in the breastes, and their heartes taken out, to offer as first fruites vnto the Idoll. The Priestes and Ministers doe consecrate this Idoll with great pomp and many Ceremonies. All the *Comarcans* and Citizens are presente at the consecration, with great triumph and incredible deuotion. After the consecration, many deuoute persons came and sticked in the dowy Image precious stones, wedges of golde, and other Jewels. After all this pomp ended, no secular man mought touche that holye Image, no nor yet come into his Chappell, nay scarcely religious persons, except they were *Tlamacaztli,* who are Priestes of order. They doe renue this Image many times wyth new dough. taking away the olde, but then blessed is hée that can get one piece of the olde ragges for relikes and chiefly for souldyers, who thought themselues sure therewith in the warres. Also at the consecration of thys Idoll, a certayne vessell of water was blessed with manye wordes and ceremonyes, and that water was preserued very religiously at the footé of the altar, for to consecrate the king when he should be crowned, and also to blesse any Captayne generall, when he shoulde be elected for the warres, with only giuing him a draught of that water.'

Hovv the Diuell appeared to the Indians.—'The Diuell did many times talke with the priestes, and with other rulers and perticular persons, but not with all sortes of men. And vnto him to whom the Diuell had appeared, was offered and presented great giftes. The wicked spirit appeared vnto them in a thousand shapes, and fashions, and

finally he was conuersant and familiar among them very
often. And the fooles thought it a greate wonder, that
Gods would be so familiar with mortal men. Yea they
not knowing that they were Diuells, and hearing of them
many things before the had hapned, gaue great credite
and beliefe to their illusions and deceits. And because
he commanded them, they sacrificed suche an infinite
number of creatures. Likewise he, vnto whom he had
appeared, carried about him painted, the likenesse wherein he shewed himself the first time. And they painted
his image vpon their dores, benches, and euery corner of
the house. And as he appeared in sundry figures and
shapes, euen so they painted him, of infinite fashions, yea
and some foule, grieslye, and fearful to beholde, but yet
vnto them, it seemed a thing delectable. So this ignorant
people giuing credite to the condemed spirite, were growen
euen to the highest hil of crueltie, vnder the coulour of
deuout and religious persons, yea they had suche a cvs-
tome, that before they would eat or drink, they wold take
thereof a little quantitie, and offer it vnto the sun and to the
earth. And if they gathered corne, fruite, or roses, they
would take a leaf before they would smel it, and offer
the same. And he that did not obserue these and suche
other ceremonies, was iudged one that had not god in his
hart, yea (as they say) a man out of the godds fauour.'

This book contains also various accounts of the immense wealth of which Mutezuma and his nobles were
possessed, which fell into the hands of the Spaniards;
gold in planches like brickbats, wedges, balls, collars,
wheels of gold, grains as they were found as large as peas,

articles both for ornament and use in war, and for the table, garnished with gold, silver, diamonds, pearls, rubies &c., which when discovered struck these greedy invaders with astonishment and sharpened their appetite for dominion and for blood. These riches were laid up in heaps in the palace of the king, for no other purpose than to be looked at; and therefore were given up freely when demanded, as useless to their possessors but greatly desired by the Spanish Monarch.

A description is given of Mexico as a place of immense population, with large wide streets and houses well built, many of them lofty, of stone, brick and wood, covered with tyles made of leaves, well lain on and forming an effectual security against both rain and heat, a conduit for bringing water from a great distance into the town, and causeways extremely well formed, with bridges on them leading to the town; which was itself placed in the centre of a large lake. Indeed the whole of this book serves to prove, that the inhabitants of the Continent, from the place where the Spaniards landed to Mexico, were in a state of complete civilization, enjoying much of the happiness of a social state holding the distinct occupations from which the enjoyments of life arise, divided among them, maintaining the different grades of society, a King, a distinct nobility, a regular priesthood, public officers, owners of large tracts of land, paying annual taxes, with labourers of all ranks and conditions. They appear to have esteemed gold and silver on no other account, than for the ornaments of their persons and their tables and temples, which were made of those metals. Their habits were regular, moderate and virtuous: a small degree of exertion furnished the means of living, and competition could scarcely be said to be known among them. But once established under a Kingly government, the love of dominion became a curse to them: wars were often lighted up, on account of the tribute which was paid to the metropolis of the empire, and revolts took place. To the westward, a country thinly peopled, the King of Mexico had an undivided sway to the shores of the Pacific; but a large portion of the country which lay between the Capital and the Gulf, which was full of people, with large and flourishing towns, was hostile to the sceptre of Montezuma, and under the influence and subject to the law of the Governor of Tlaxcallan. This unhappy division of power, and the bitter jealousy which had long been cherished by the two prevailing governments, were the cause of the final subjugation of the capital of the kingdom. Without them it would have been impossible for the small army of Spaniards which invaded them to have formed an establishment in the country; still less to have maintained their authority, after it had been discovered by the Indians, that the only purpose for which they came was plunder. These men first obtained an influence among the natives, through that extreme simplicity and character of mildness by which they were marked, and it was afterwards cherished and confirmed by the jealousies which they carefully fermented, the false hopes by which they fed the discontented party, the promises always unfulfilled which were liberally given, and the cruel severity which they exercised as soon as they had gained a footing firm enough to empower them to use decisive measures. Nor did they finally succeed without the almost entire annihilation of the higher orders of the people, the princes, the priests and leading men, and tens of thousands, perhaps I might say, hundreds of thousands of the gentle, harmless, virtuous Indians. Of these conquerors it might indeed be said, that " they created a desart and called it Peace;" and the terror with which they inspired the feeble natives, like that which surrounded the dungeons of the Inquisition, sealed every mouth which still remained unclosed in silence, and brought every neck to a yoke galling, sore, and insupportable, under which millions more sunk into an early grave, welcome to their broken hearts.

CHAPTER XII.

AND now, my Reader, we will take a general view of the contents of this volume, in order to ascertain the value of the information that has been afforded from various, but all, I believe, respectable quarters, and how far it may be seen to prove the point for which it has been collected; namely, that the original inhabitants of America are descended in a direct and pure line from the Ten Tribes of Israel.

If we respect the prophetic language of the Old Testament, we are compelled to believe that the people of God, who once enjoyed special tokens of his favour and lost them, as foretold by their great prophet and lawgiver, in consequence of disobedience, will be restored to his favour and regain the distinction they once enjoyed. If any confirmation of this sacred truth were required, it is obtained from the actual state of the Jews, the descendants of the two tribes of Judah and Benjamin, who are still living in a state of separation from all the nations among whom they dwell, adhering stricktly to the worship of their One and Only God, and exhibiting a faithfulness of worship that does honour to Him they serve. Here they are among us still waiting for their redemption. And it is a thought, unaccompained by doubt in the Christian's mind, that their day of salvation draweth near, when they shall be united with us in the worship of their God and King.

But why they, two tribes alone, and not the other ten, who are all included in the general charter, of whom scripture speaks in the plainest terms, and calls them by name? Are they not also to be recovered and restored, together with the Jews? Yes, they are to be so. Not *the scattered* and *dispersed* alone, but also the *outcast* shall return to the Almighty's embrace and to their own land. For, as Paul assures us. *All Israel shall be saved.*

These tribes have therefore an existence some where— far from their brethren; who *are ignorant of them* and now *acknowledge them not.*

One of their own prophets has told us the way in which they departed from their captivity. In the book of Esdras their journey can be traced into *a land where no man dwelt.* And although throughout the space of two thousand five hundred years *they have not been enquired after,* they are not less in being on this account. In that direction which the prophetic historian points out, *a way of a year and a half's journey,* is a passage to a wide land, *wherein they might wander* undisturbed *from sea to sea.* In that land an immense population has been discovered, in their usages and customs unlike any of the tribes and nations existing in Europe or Asia, with peculiar and striking features, which render them remarkable. Of these let the following be duly considered.

They are living in tribes, with heads of tribes—they have all a family likeness, though covering thousands of leagues of land; and have a tradition prevailing universally, that they came into that country at the North-West corner—they are a very religious people, and yet have entirely escaped the idolatry of the old world—they acknowledge One God, the Great Spirit, who created all things seen and unseen—the name by which this being is known to them is *ale*, the old Hebrew name of God; he is also called *yehowah*, sometimes *yah*, and also *abba*—for this Great Being they profess a high reverence, calling him the head of their community, and themselves his favorite people—they believe that he was more favorable to them in old times than he is now, that their fathers were in covenant with him, that he talked with them and gave them laws—they are distinctly heard to sing with their religious dances, *halleluyah* or praise to *jah*: other remarkable sounds go out of their mouths, as *shilu-yo, shilu-he, ale-yo, he-wah, yohewah*: but they profess not to know the meaning of these words; only that they learned to use them upon sacred occasions—they acknowledge the government of a providence over-ruling all things, and express a willing submission to whatever takes place—they keep annual feasts which resemble those of the Mosaic ritual; a feast of first fruits, which they do not permit themselves to taste until they have made an offering of them to God; also an evening festival, in which no bone of the animal that is eaten may be broken; and if one family be not large enough to consume the whole of it, a neighbouring family is called in to assist: the whole of it is consumed, and the relics are burned before the rising of the next day's sun: there is one part of the animal which they never eat, the hollow part of the thigh—they eat bitter vegetables and observe severe fasts, for the purpose of cleansing themselves from sin—they have also a feast of harvest, when their fruits are gathered in, a daily sacrifice and a feast of love—their forefathers practised the right of circumcision; but not knowing why so strange a practice was continued, and not approving of it, they gave it up—there is a sort of jubilee kept by some of them—they have cities of refuge, to which a guilty man and even a murderer may fly and be safe; for these beloved or sacred towns are never defiled by the shedding of blood—in their temples is a holy place into which none may enter but the priest, and he only on particular occasions—there he makes a yearly atonement for sin, dressed in a fantastic garb, which is a humble imitation of the High Priest's robes, with a breast plate and other ornaments—he addresses the people in the *old divine speech* and calls them *the beloved and holy people*—they have a succession of priests, who are inducted into office by purification and anointing—they had once a holy book, which while they kept, things went well with them; they lost it, and in consequence of the loss fell under the displeasure of the Great Spirit; but they believe they shall one day regain it—they are looking for and expecting some one to come and teach them the right way.—

Let the reader here peruse Amos 8, 11, and Ezekiel 37. Their forefathers had a power of foretelling future events and working miracles—they have an ark or chest, in which they keep their holy things, and which they carry with them to the wars—a person is appointed to carry it, called the Priest for the war, who is especially purified by fasting and taking a bitter drink—he has a sagan or helper: no other than these two dare to touch the ark, not even an enemy—it must not be placed on the ground, through fear of defilement, but upon a heap of stones piled up, or on a wooden stool provided for the purpose—all the males appear in their temples three times a year at the appointed feasts: on which occasions the women and children do not form any part of the devotional body—their temples are high places: among the more civilized they were huge heaps of earth, used as places to bury their dead as well as for temples, altars and religious worship; to which they last resorted when driven by an enemy, and where no quarter was either received or given—they tell us, that God made the first man of clay and breathed on him, and so gave him life; of a flood in which all the inhabitants of the earth were drowned except one family, which was saved in a large vessel with various animals; that a great bird and a little one were sent out from it, that the little one returned with a branch in his mouth but the great one remained abroad—they speak of a confusion of tongues when new languages were first formed; and that men once lived till their feet were worn out with walking and their throats with eating—at one of their feasts twelve beloved men are employed to form

a booth or tent of green branches, in which they perform
certain religious rites, raise an altar of twelve stones, on
which no tool is allowed to be used, and on it they offer
twelve sacrifices; a feast much resembling the feast of
tabernacles—some of them have ten men and ten stones—
at death their beloved people sleep, and go to their fathers;
they wash and anoint the bodies, and hire mourners to shed
tears and lament over them—in affliction they lay their
hand on their mouths and their mouths in the dust—they
separate with singular care their women when under
peculiar circumstances, both the young unmarried ones
and the wives; with the latter of whom they abstain from
communication during war, and for some days before and
after—they have laws of uncleanness in other cases, as unclean animals which they never eat, and a careful avoidance
of every thing unclean—time is reckoned by them in the
manner of the ancient Hebrews, and their years begin at
the same season—in their language are an abundance of
words similar to the Hebrew ones, and it is generally constructed in the manner of that language—their ancient
works, raised at very remote periods, are of immense size
and large extent, and the more interesting, because they
offer the proof, that these people were by no means unacquainted with arts and science: they have an evident
affinity to the public works and vast structures of Egypt
and of Palestine; the same hands may be thought to have
raised the Pyramids of the old and of the new world, the
same superstition to have marked their places of sepulture,
and the same creed to have been the rule of their lives
both as to time and a hereafter.

It is not pretended that all these remarkable usages, customs and thoughts, are found alike in all the parts of the vast continent of America. Some of the fragments of an ancient system have been discovered in one place, and some in another. Many of them, and the most important to our present purpose, are found to prevail among many or all of the nations that have been best known: and it will now be judged, whether there be not a greater plausibility in the supposition maintained in the foregoing pages, than in the attempt which has been again and again made to shew that these nations are of Tartar origin. Among the Tartars none of those pecularities are discovered which bring the American Indians so near to a Hebrew origin; and, without entering deeper into the investigation, I shall take leave of my reader with the persuasion, that he has not been uninterested and uninstructed by the perusal of this little volume.

FINIS.

PRINTED BY W. W. ARLISS, PLYMOUTH.

AMERICA AND THE HOLY LAND

An Arno Press Collection

Adler, Cyrus and Aaron M. Margalith. **With Firmness in the Right:** American Diplomatic Action Affecting Jews, 1840-1945.   1946

Babcock, Maltbie Davenport. **Letters From Egypt and Palestine.**   1902

Badt-Strauss, Bertha. **White Fire:** The Life and Works of Jessie Sampter.   1956

Barclay, J[ames] T[urner]. **The City of the Great King.**   1858

Baron, Salo W. and Jeanette M. Baron. **Palestinian Messengers in America, 1849-79.**   1943

Bartlett, S[amuel] C[olcord]. **From Egypt to Palestine.**   1879

Bliss, Frederick Jones. **The Development of Palestine Exploration.** 1907

Bond, Alvan. **Memoir of the Rev. Pliny Fisk, A. M.:** Late Missionary to Palestine.   1828

Browne, J[ohn] Ross. **Yusef:** Or the Journey of the Frangi.   1853

Burnet, D[avid] S[taats], compiler. **The Jerusalem Mission:** Under the Direction of the American Christian Missionary Society.   1853

Call to America to Build Zion.   1977

Christian Protagonists for Jewish Restoration.   1977

Cox, Samuel S. **Orient Sunbeams:** Or, From the Porte to the Pyramids, By Way of Palestine.   1882

Cresson, Warder. **The Key of David.**   1852

Crossman, Richard. **Palestine Mission: A Personal Record.**   1947

Davis, Moshe, editor. **Israel:** Its Role in Civilization.   1956

De Hass, Frank S. **Buried Cities Recovered:** Or, Explorations in Bible Lands.   1883

[Even, Charles]. **The Lost Tribes of Israel:** Or, The First of the Red Men. 1861

Field, Frank McCoy. **Where Jesus Walked:** Through the Holy Land with the Master.   1951

Fink, Reuben, editor. **America and Palestine:** The Attitude of Official America and of the American People.   1944

Fosdick, Harry Emerson. **A Pilgrimage to Palestine.**   1927

Fulton, John. **The Beautiful Land:** Palestine, Historical, Geographical and Pictorial.   1891

Gilmore, Albert Field. **East and West of Jordan.**   1929

Gordon, Benjamin L[ee]. **New Judea:** Jewish Life in Modern Palestine and Egypt.   1919

Holmes, John Haynes. **Palestine To-Day and To-Morrow:** A Gentile's Survey of Zionism.   1929

Holy Land Missions and Missionaries.   1977

[Hoofien, Sigfried]. **Report of Mr. S. Hoofien to the Joint Distribution Committee of the American Funds for Jewish War Sufferers.**   1918

Intercollegiate Zionist Association of America. **Kadimah.**   1918

Isaacs, Samuel Hillel. **The True Boundaries of the Holy Land.**   1917

Israel, J[ohn] and H[enry] Lundt. **Journal of a Cruize in the U. S. Ship Delaware 74 in the Mediterranean in the Years 1833 & 34.**   1835

Johnson, Sarah Barclay. **Hadji in Syria:** Or, Three Years in Jerusalem.   1858

Kallen, Horace M[eyer]. **Frontiers of Hope.**   1929

Krimsky, Jos[eph]. **Pilgrimage & Service.**   1918-1919

Kyle, Melvin Grove. **Excavating Kirjath-Sepher's Ten Cities.**   1934

Kyle, Melvin Grove. **Explorations at Sodom:** The Story of Ancient Sodom in the Light of Modern Research.   1928

Lipsky, Louis. **Thirty Years of American Zionism.**   1927

Lynch, W[illiam] F[rancis]. **Narrative of the United States' Expedition to the River Jordan and the Dead Sea.**   1849

Macalister, R[obert] A[lexander] S[tewart]. **A Century of Excavation in Palestine.**   [1925]

McCrackan, W[illiam] D[enison]. **The New Palestine.**   1922

Merrill, Selah. **Ancient Jerusalem.**   1908

Meyer, Isidore S., editor. **Early History of Zionism in America.**   1958

Miller, Ellen Clare. **Eastern Sketches:** Notes of Scenery, Schools, and Tent Life in Syria and Palestine.   1871

[Minor, Clorinda]. **Meshullam!** Or, Tidings From Jerusalem.   1851

Morris, Robert. **Freemasonry in the Holy Land.**   1872

Morton, Daniel O[liver]. **Memoir of Rev. Levi Parsons, Late Missionary to Palestine.** 1824

Odenheimer, W[illiam] H. **Jerusalem and its Vicinity.** 1855

Olin, Stephen. **Travels in Egypt, Arabia Petraea, and the Holy Land.** 1843. Two Vols. in One

Palmer, E[dward] H[enry]. **The Desert of the Exodus.** 1871. Two Vols. in One

Paton, Lewis Bayles. **Jerusalem in Bible Times.** 1908

Pioneer Settlement in the Twenties. 1977

Prime, William C[ooper]. **Tent Life in the Holy Land.** 1857

Rifkind, Simon H., et al. **The Basic Equities of the Palestine Problem.** 1947

Rix, Herbert. **Tent and Testament:** A Camping Tour in Palestine with Some Notes on Scriptural Sites. 1907

Robinson, Edward. **Biblical Researches in Palestine, Mount Sinai and Arabia Petraea.** 1841. Three Volumes

Robinson, Edward. **Later Biblical Researches in Palestine and in Adjacent Regions.** 1856

Schaff, Philip. **Through Bible Lands:** Notes on Travel in Egypt, the Desert, and Palestine. [1878]

Smith, Ethan. **View of the Hebrews.** 1823

Smith, George A[lbert], et al. **Correspondence of Palestine Tourists.** 1875

Smith, Henry B[oynton] and Roswell D. Hitchcock. **The Life, Writings and Character of Edward Robinson.** 1863

Sneersohn, H[aym] Z[vee]. **Palestine and Roumania.** 1872

Szold, Henrietta. **Recent Jewish Progress in Palestine.** 1915

Talmage, T[homas] de Witt. **Talmage on Palestine:** A Series of Sermons. 1890

Taylor, Bayard. **The Lands of the Saracen:** Or, Pictures of Palestine, Asia Minor, Sicily, and Spain. 1855

The American Republic and Ancient Israel. 1977

Thompson, George, et al. **A View of the Holy Land.** 1850

Van Dyke, Henry. **Out-of-Doors in the Holy Land:** Impressions of Travel in Body and Spirit. 1908

Vester, Bertha [Hedges] Spafford. **Our Jerusalem:** An American Family in the Holy City, 1881-1949.   1950

Wallace, Edwin Sherman. **Jerusalem the Holy.**   1898

[Ware, William] . **Julian:** Or Scenes in Judea.   1841. Two Vols. in One

Worsley, Israel. **A View of the American Indians:** Showing Them to Be the Descendants of the Ten Tribes of Israel.   1828

Yehoash [Bloomgarden, Solomon] . **The Feet of the Messenger.**   1923